To Carl Kraag and Valter Fabiani,
with much love

John Fleming
and
Hugh Honour

Remembered

by

Susanna Johnston

GIBSON SQUARE

This edition published by Gibson Square for the first time

UK   Tel: +44 (0)20 7096 1100
US   Tel: +1 646 216 9813

        info@gibsonsquare.com
        www.gibsonsquare.com

        ISBN   9781783341115
        eISBN   9781783341122

Papers used by Gibson Square are natural, recyclable products made from wood grown in sustainable forests; inks used are vegetable based. Manufacturing conforms to ISO 14001, and is accredited to FSC and PEFC chain of custody schemes. Colour-printing is through a certified CarbonNeutral® company that offsets its CO2 emissions.

Contents

Introduction	7
1	11
2	15
3	21
4	25
5	29
6	33
7	37
8	45
9	49
10	55
11	63
12	75

13	81
14	87
15	97
16	107
17	117
18	129
19	139
20	149
21	159
22	165
23	169
24	175
25	179
Postscripts	187

Introduction

'Well' John and Hugh might have said, had they heard that I planned to write this memoir, 'Don't do it. We are of no interest whatsoever.'

On May 19th 2016, our good friend, Valter Fabiani rang me early one morning to tell me that Hugh had died in the night. For many months I had jumped when Valter rang – both fearing and hoping for that news. Hugh so wanted for it all to be over. Later that day Darryl Pinckney telephoned from New York to commiserate. Hugh and I had been very close friends for nearly sixty years and I was tearful. Darryl said 'Look Zanna. Why don't you write about your friendship with John and Hugh. It was an unusual and wonderful one.' I started the same day. Just shreds and snatches. Memories of our times with Percy Lubbock in Lerici in the 1950s. Later in London and Lucca. I barely mention John and Hugh's achievements. They are so well documented that I leave them alone in this, entirely, personal memoir. Contact with Hugh, towards the end, would not have been possible without the warmth and help of Hugh's '*erede*' Valter Fabiani – who kept me in close touch with Hugh (messages to and fro) – when distance and talking to him on the telephone made it difficult. Dates and times have often eluded me, in spite of the somewhat irregular diaries I have kept throughout the years. I now, whatever their assumed reaction, offer John and Hugh this scatty memoir with respect and love.

Whenever I read *Pride and Prejudice* – about once a year – I always think, when I come to Elizabeth Bennet's much quoted remark, of John and Hugh. 'I hope I never ridicule what is wise or good. Follies and nonsense, whims and inconsistencies, *do* divert me I own, and I laugh at them whenever I can...' But they would have said 'we' instead of 'I'.

Now, to my intense happiness, it is decided that future generations of my family will own and spend much time in the Villa that John and Hugh rescued, recreated and lived in so fruitfully and indefatigably.

Many thanks to Antony Beevor, Harry Mount, Sarah Riddell, Alexander Chancellor, Carl Kraag, Valter Fabiani, Selina Hastings, Justin Gowers, Richard and Hatty Dorment, Mollie and John Julius Norwich, Nic and Sukie Paravicini, Julia Mount, Fram Dinshaw, Claudia Fitzherbert, Rudolf Loewenstein, Jaco and Kate Schoeman, Fiona Wright, John and Caroline Lucas-Tooth, Linda Kelly, Alissa Rams, Martin Rynja, my four daughters, Clara, Lily, Rose and Silvy, and most of all to my husband Nicky.

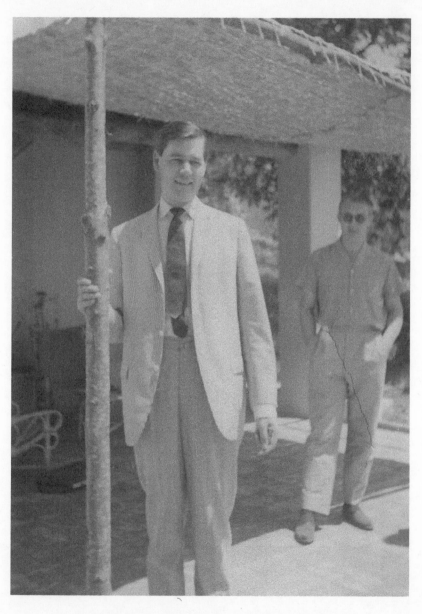

John Fleming and Hugh Honour at their first home, 1950s

1

This memoir is about my long and life-enriching friendship with John Fleming and Hugh Honour. Nonetheless I feel I must start it by saying a little of myself – how I lived at the time and the strange set of circumstances that led me to them. It was 1957. I was twenty-one and, for no particularly good reason, perched in Rome. Very lost. Very broke. No boyfriend, no sense of direction, no qualifications, no ambition other than a yearning to stay in Italy. I moved into a crowded house in Trastevere. It was lived in by Nigel Ryan, Anthony Rouse, and a number of other friends. None of them quite knew what to do with me when I couldn't pay my share of the rent – but they were kind. At home, my sister was married and my brothers were – well – boys and better catered for than I was. My father considered me to be a problem. Much, much later I read some frightful things he had said about me to Jim Lees-Milne. Jim quoted them word for word in his published diaries. 'My daughter, Susanna, has given me no pleasure whatsoever,' my father had said.

One evening I went with my gang of friends to dine in a *trattoria*. We were joined there by a somewhat older man. He was fifty five or so, very sympathetic and reassuring with tufty hair and tweedy clothes. His name was Gordon Waterfield. He, a distinguished broadcaster, changed everything for me. I sat beside him and poured my troubles out; my fear of returning to London, my indigence; my longing to live in Italy. He wrote my telephone number down on a paper table napkin and said that he would ponder on my problems and promised to ring me in the morning.

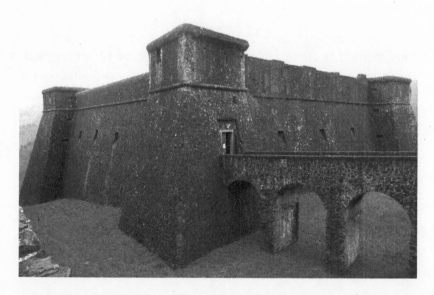

Gordon Waterfield's Fortezza della Brunella in Aulla

He was true to his word and rang the next day. I bundled down the dirty stairway to the telephone in the mood for inducement. He thought that he might have found a solution; not necessarily a hundred per cent satisfactory one – no guarantee that it would come off – but worth a try.

He told me to pack a bag and said that he would fetch me in an hour. On the drive northwards from Rome, my new friend outlined plans. Oddly enough I did not feel in any way shy or awkward with him. He was taking me to a castle that he owned in Aulla. It had belonged to his parents, Aubrey and Lina Waterfield, who bought it in the 1920's – having rented it for many years. Aubrey had first seen the castle in 1896 when still up at Oxford and whilst walking there from Portofino. Gordon said that it was a wonderful place but was fast becoming an albatross. At present, he had to let it for most of the year but the outgoings were enormous and the rent didn't bring in nearly enough to cover the costs. He couldn't charge much from tenants as the house was in poor condition. The drive took about six hours and, during those hours, he told me more. I was to stay for a few nights at the albatross and he was to make telephone calls on my behalf. He made it mysterious but I trusted him.

As we drove into the noisy town of Aulla I saw, on a hill, rising up above us and seemingly embedded in the cliff face, an ancient castellated building. We drove in at valley level, wound up around the back of the hill and parked on a gravel space at the top. Along one side was a wall with a door in it. When we pushed it open we found ourselves in a garden – very overgrown. We walked across the garden and into a shed. Inside the shed was a flight of stairs leading down. It reminded me of *Alice in Wonderland* as we entered this ancient building from the top; starting at roof level and making our way down the staircase to a series of big, beautiful and faded rooms from which you could see the town down below. The main view was scored with railway lines – part of a marshalling yard. It was noisy and rough down there. Indoors the wiring inspired little confidence. The house was on the brink of collapse.

At supper on a terrace, Gordon filled me in a little more. In the morning he was going to make another telephone call. Not far from Aulla, near Lerici and beside the sea, lived an old, blind Englishman. A man of letters. His name was Percy Lubbock and for many years he had relied on a series of younger Englishmen to live in the house as his companion and amanuensis – to read aloud to him; write letters, filter visitors and so on. Gordon put emphasis on the word Englishman. No woman had ever held the post. At that time Percy had two 'readers.' They were called John Fleming and Hugh Honour. They had been there for three or four years and were now longing to escape but were not prepared to leave Percy in the lurch. They had searched desperately for a substitute and Gordon hoped that he had come up with one. I had never heard of Percy Lubbock.

For me, so many years later, the day before I met John and Hugh is a vital part of my memory of them.

2

Gordon drove me to Percy Lubbock's house, Gli Scafari (the brigands) in the morning. He said that he had little instinct as to the outcome of our adventure. He had left a message with Elena, the maid, who had a sweet character but a weak intellect. 'John and Hugh will be the ones to decide' Gordon said. 'Percy is certain to be prejudiced against employing a girl.' He looked at me a trifle anxiously, or so I thought – but it was a bit late in the day for that. Maybe he wondered if my stripey trousers, colourful shirt, lipstick and earrings might tell against me – not that Percy would be able to see them – but John and Hugh?

Busses seemed almost to have taken over the road as they honked around curves, horns in constant use – so sharp were the bends. As we neared Gli Scafari, Gordon told me that his father

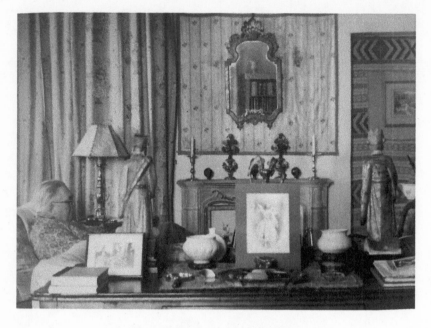

Percy Lubbock at Gli Scafari, 1950s

Aubrey had first spotted the site on which the house was built when his friends, D. H. Lawrence and Frieda lived a couple of miles across the bay at Fiascherino. It was there that Lawrence wrote first drafts of two of his most famous novels – *The Rainbow* and *Women in Love*. Aubrey Waterfield had tipped the Lubbocks off when they were known to be searching for a site in the area. We drove in past a lodge, half hidden in clusters of white wisteria, and dropped down towards a promontory at the end of which stood the house that overlooked a sheltered bay. It was large and rambling and gave a sea-side impression of arches and loggias. It was July and the bay was calm. On the doorstep stood three figures. Statues awaiting us. John Fleming wearing chef's trousers that spilled over sandals, a loose shirt and strong spectacles that glinted in the bright

16

sun. Hugh Honour, handsome, taller, younger than John and more conventionally dressed in a linen coat and white trousers. He smoked a thin cigarette that smelled of Turkish tobacco. They were, respectively, about thirty five and twenty seven at the time. Both looked hopefully welcoming until they caught sight of me when barely disguised shock almost overtook them. I'm not sure that John didn't whisper 'mercy' as he took note of my appearance. The small, slitty-eyed maid, Elena, who stood with them, however, screeched 'it's a *Signorina*. I believed *Signor* Waterfield to say he was bringing a *Signorino*.' John and Hugh remained calmly polite though clearly bemused as they led me and Gordon into a shady marble hall. A wide staircase wound out of the darkness to the sunny first floor where the rooms led onto a series of loggias – kept cool by flapping awnings and canvas curtains. 'The boys,' as John and Hugh were then often known, decided that Gordon was to introduce me to Percy while they hovered nearby until the interview was over.

All in a trice we were there – in Percy Lubbock's book lined study where he spent his days. He sat, flabby and wearing a dressing-gown, glass to his lips.

From a vast arm chair, he held up his hand in greeting. 'My dear Gordon. You bring me help, I hear. I am most grateful. Where is he? I didn't catch his name earlier. Introduce me.'

I hung back. Gordon replied 'Percy. I'm afraid the message was incorrectly conveyed. I have a young lady with me. Susanna. Susanna Chancellor.'

'I don't think that will do at all. Dear me no. Not at all.'

'Wait a bit Percy. She's prepared to act as stop-gap. John and Hugh, as you know, can't stay much longer. She'll help you with letters and so forth – even if you don't care to be read to by a

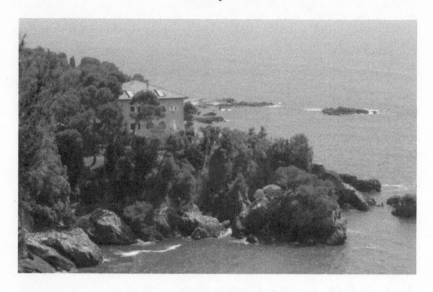

Gli Scafari, Lerici

woman. I'm certain she can be of use.'

I shook Percy Lubbock's damp hand and, immediately, rather liked him. He looked gentle. Mercifully he could not see me.

Gordon settled to chat to Percy. They were, after all, old friends – even if Gordon was unlikely to have solved the problem of who was going to read to him. I looked around the room and had the impression that everything in it was pleasing. Nothing jarred and it conveyed a cosiness that was unknown in Italian houses; literary magazines, rugs, pictures, cushions and old world ornaments. A vast terracotta Buddha, not unlike its owner, sat on a gold-handled chest.

I guessed, and rightly as it turned out, that John and Hugh stood together in the passage wondering what on earth to make of me and whether I could possibly, conceivably 'do.' A substitute reader was of vital importance to them and they were having to summon

18

up a degree of flexibility that was unusual in their scheme of things. They had read, in turns of course, to Percy for several years. Hugh had been writing exhibition reviews for *The Times*, had become a special Italian correspondent for *The Conoisseur*, had contributed many articles to *Country Life* and researched his first major book, *Chinoiserie: The Vision of Cathay*. He had also, not long before, published a long essay on Horace Walpole for a series commissioned by The British Council and the National Book League for writers and their works. John plotted his book – *Robert Adam and his Circle*. Both needed more time for their enterprises.

Life at Lerici had cost them nothing. They had managed to save enough to live independently of Percy and planned to rent a Villino from Freya Stark at Asolo where they would be nearer to the libraries and treasures of Venice. All they needed was to release

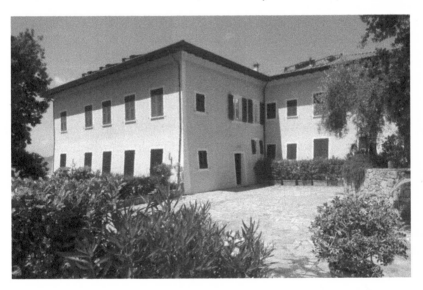

Gli Scafari, Lerici

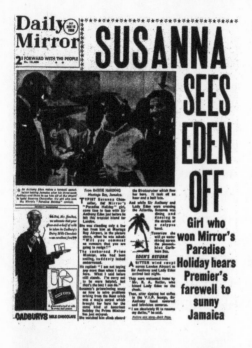

Front page: 'Will you resign Prime Minister?'

themselves from Gli Scafari and the pressures of their ageing, blind employer.

There was another, more urgent, problem. The house they had taken at Asolo was not to be free for several months. Whoever succeeded them would have to become their constant companion since Percy was letting them stay there until they were able to move. The hope was of course that, once relieved of their daily duties, they would be able to continue with their own increasingly numerous tasks. Would this jazzy looking girl fill the bill? Had she ever heard of Walter Pater or read Froude's *Life of Carlyle*?

It all depended on what happened during lunch which was to be served to all five of us on the loggia. Gordon Waterfield was to stay until the afternoon and then, whatever the outcome, to take me back to Aulla for a day or two. From there, if things went in the unexpected direction, I would return to Rome to collect my few possessions, say goodbye to my room mates and head back for Gli Scafari to find myself in the company of three scholarly men who were clearly all horrified by the prospect of being cooped up with a young and probably flighty girl.

Lunch on the loggia was served by Alfredo who was always white gloved. He and Maria (his wife) were enjoying the joke. A young lady indeed! Gordon sat beside Percy. I did too – with John Fleming on my other side. Hugh sat opposite me. As Gordon tried to convince Percy to take me on, I turned to John. He was inquisitive, almost cheeky, and asked me many questions. That was a help. I enjoyed his curiosity and told him of my recent and peculiar experiences. The year before I had won a holiday for two in Jamaica by entering a competition in the *Daily Mirror* about how to solve the Suez crisis and had been widely known, for several weeks, as the *Daily Mirror* Paradise Holiday Girl. John stretched his eyes. He then asked me what I had read recently. I told him that I was very much enjoying *The Card*. A spark on that subject set us both off into laughter. Even Hugh looked hopeful and something came alive between us all. They both, it transpired, approved of Arnold Bennett's novels. I'm not sure if I quite realised it at the time but a flame had been ignited and it continued to burn brightly for many decades. I heard Percy say to Gordon 'If John and Hugh say so – but only for a short time. Only until we can find someone better suited.'

It suddenly seemed to be settled. I heard John say to Hugh, 'it might be rather fun.' (Not that Hugh particularly liked 'fun') They came to the front door as Gordon and I prepared to leave. Hugh said 'We both much look forward to seeing you here again very soon.'

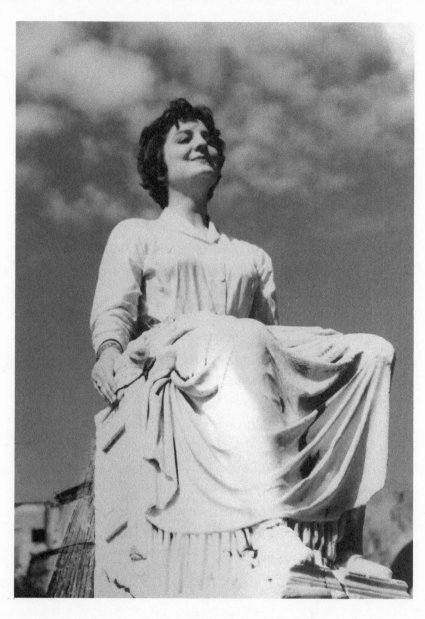

Susanna in Rome, just before meeting John and Hugh

3

John and Hugh met me at La Spezia station on a stupefyingly hot afternoon. Hugh drove (John couldn't) in a small black Fiat that they jointly owned. Hugh was stately, anxious and polite. John appeared excited. Running in tandem with his intellectual, bachelor side – he clearly had a weakness for what he called 'high jinks.' Maybe I slipped into the 'high jinks' slot.

They drove me through the pretty town of Lerici – pointing out the ancient tower and telling me that Percy Bysshe Shelley had drowned there. John did most of the talking and Hugh added scholarly comments. Later Hugh wrote me a description of the area which can't be bettered so I'm going to leave the absorbing subject and will allow him to take over in due course.

As we neared the villa, John said, 'We feel we must tell you that

Percy may not give you much of a welcome. We will though.'
Neither of the boys, then or later, ever used the personal pronoun
'I.'

'We' was what they always said.

Hugh warned 'Percy is very resistant to women in spite of non-
stop rambling about his ghastly dead wife, Lady Sybil. Very
important to remember the "Lady" bit.' John chipped in 'But he'll
take to you pretty soon. Not at once, I daresay. You won't see him
until supper time. Elena will take you to your room and tomorrow
we'll show you the ropes.' One of them added, 'you have a clear
voice, suited to reading aloud – and it's old fashioned – Percy is
deeply traditional in many ways in spite of claiming to be a
communist. He likes a bit of background.'

Back at the villa, Elena, beaming at the prospect of someone
new to talk to, showed me to a celestial bedroom. Marble basin,
four poster bed with mosquito netting clipped back. A desk, ink
bottle, writing paper and blotter. Prints, arm chairs covered in a
fading William Morris pattern. No sight of the sea but Corsican
pines, olive and ilex trees filled the entire view from the window –
glittering in sunlight.

Elena's slitty eyes cascaded with puss and she wiped them non-
stop. My Italian was poor but just good enough for conversational
purposes. She was happy to have female company in the house –
other than that of Maria, the unkind cook – and helped me unpack
with zeal. Her *'fidanzato'*, Dante, a local hunchback, had suffered
once more in a recent storm. It had been too rough for fish but
more sea-horses had been washed up on the shore. Shoals of them.
She took several out of her pocket and presented them to me as
she wiped her eyes. Tiny, perfectly formed, curving and dry sea

horses. I wish I'd kept them. Poor Elena went on 'Dante is not allowed into the kitchen any more. Maria says he smells of fish. But, *Signorina*, he is a fisherman.'

The four of us, Percy, John, Hugh and I, met before supper in Percy's study. None of it, including Percy, had quite come into focus for me at that stage. He had to be helped into the room by a sulky male nurse, Aldo, who threw him into a chair as he shuddered and muttered. Grudgingly, he asked one of the boys to offer me a drink. Vinegary white wine. Nobody spoke much until supper when, again, Alfredo crept round serving an omelette. Percy insisted on an egg dish at every meal. John and Hugh struggled as I sat silent and Percy muttered, 'Oh dear me no. She won't do at all. Not at all.' John whispered that Percy was, by now, very drunk and advised me to take no notice. John's eyes twinkled and Hugh gave me kind smiles.

After supper we had to listen to a military march by Mahler that Hugh plopped onto a wind-up gramophone. Then Aldo came to take Percy, shambling and complaining about me, to bed.

'No idea. Oh dear me no. She hasn't got the faintest idea', he groaned – a much repeated phrase – but, luckily, fading out before too long.

After Percy went to bed we all settled down for a long and more than enjoyable chat and I knew I was to be happy there.

John and Hugh, when they wished me good night said, in unison 'We are both very pleased to have you here and, we're certain, Percy soon will be too.'

4

I would have been dismayed and deterred had it not been for the friendliness of John and Hugh. No sooner had Percy gone to bed that first evening than the underlying anxiety of the situation began to slip away and the boys appeared to be enjoying themselves. I re-lived it all as I dressed the following morning. Sometimes they had spoken together, sometimes separately but always handing the conversation seamlessly to each other.

One of them pointed to the chimney piece and drew my attention to a transparent jar half filled with specks of ash. 'Those are the remains of *Lady* Sybil.' Then the fun began. They told me much of the history of this unusual place.

'Percy', one of them said, probably John, 'of course is

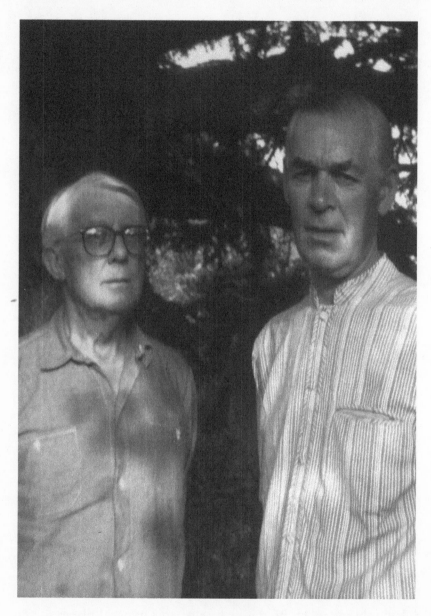

John and Hugh

queer.' (They always used that word.) That Percy was 'queer' had not occurred to me.

I learnt the following.

His had, presumably, been a *mariage blanc* – Percy having always preferred gentlemen to ladies. Neither of them had been young when they married. Lady Sybil had more or less lassoed Percy when Geoffrey Scott (who she was married to at the time) – author of The *Architecture of Humanism* and *The Portrait of Zelide* – tired of her. When, in fact, he could stand her no more. John remembered a story of a scene in a church in Florence where a memorial service was being held. Halfway through it Sybil whimpered, 'Geoffrey. I'm going to faint.' He shouted, 'All right Sybil. Faint if that's what you want.'

She had been born Sybil Cuffe. Her father was an Irish peer called Lord Desart – but he was not rich and Sybil was plain. It had been imperative to see her well married and it must have been a relief when a prosperous American called Bayard Cutting came along. One daughter was born to them before Bayard's early death from tuberculosis. The daughter, it transpired, was Iris Origo – the well known writer and present owner of the house in which we all lived in luxury.

Percy and Sybil came back to the bay just after the second war which they had spent, for safety's sake, in Switzerland. They had built the house in the late 1920s not long after they were married. The architect was Cecil Pinsent who did much rarefied work in Italy and the decorator was Sybil Colefax – then at the start of her great career.

John and Hugh produced the theory that his wife had actually caused Percy to lose his sight by insisting that he read to her far into the night using a pencil torch (anything brighter brought on one of her headaches.) One night, or so they had heard, she was aggravated by the noise of a dog barking by the shore and sent Percy out to shoot it. He, of course, pacifist and aesthete that he was, had no gun and had to rouse the gardener to do it for him.

We talked and laughed until Hugh said, 'we must go to bed – but more in the morning.' It was then that they delivered their endearing first-night message.

Breakfast was brought to us in our rooms but we had planned to meet in the same spot before Percy was trundled through to join us the following morning. I couldn't remember when I'd laughed so much and longed, immediately, to see them again.

5

I was excited. Had it been friendship at first sight? I felt so. Certainly with John. I was less confident about the dignified and slightly wary Hugh – although I had taken to him hugely.

Hugh was working and I met John, the first time I had seen him on his own, in Percys' study. I sneaked a peep at Lady Sybil's ashes and we both laughed.

'Now' he said 'a bit of preparation before Percy joins us in an hour or so. Alfredo will come in with the post – on a silver tray. Air Mail edition of *The Times*. Periodicals (some very left wing), letters from hopeful relations who don't realise that this place belongs to Iris Origo. The letters you will have to deal with and answer by hand. The periodicals aren't too difficult as he can't see and you will be able to pick and choose.' He assured me that there would be a break for lunch 'when, for the time being, we will be there too.'

Rest after lunch and 'heavy' reading in the early afternoon. Although a determined atheist, Percy was interested in theology. Sometimes he liked to listen to verses from the Bible and chapters from Albert Schweitzer's *'Paul's Realism versus Symbolism.'* Here, as he spoke, John took off his spectacles, smiled and said with some amusement 'I don't know if you'll enjoy that much.'

'Light' reading after tea, was likely to consist of Henry James, Edith Wharton (once a close friend of Percy's, as had been Henry James). Sometimes, and surprisingly, Agatha Christie. 'He likes the works of Thackeray too', John added. *'The Adventures of Philip* and *The Newcomes* in particular.' I had never heard of either of them – *Vanity Fair* was as far as I'd got.

John suggested that he do the job that morning as I watched and listened. Percy was hauled into his chair, after which he ignored my presence, and I took stock as John managed affairs.

Shelves, lining each wall of the room, bulged with books. A plaid rug that was supposed to cover him – slipped and Percy's dressing gown fell open – leaving his gargantuan white belly bare. Two mauve, podgy feet spilled over the sides of velvet slippers and the neck of a bottle glinted from under his arm chair. How, I wondered, did he collect and conceal bottles – blind as a bat? Maybe an 'arrangement' with the male nurse. On a small mahogany table, near to where he sat, was planted his official ration. This was a carafe of warm white Elba wine which stood beside a glass and a plate of salted almonds. His round face flopped into the folds of his chest as it fell to and fro.

That first morning there were no letters but John read aloud from Sir Stephen King Hall's pacifist news letter. Percy, having been a conscientious objector during the First War, agreed with every syllable of it. John told me that he, too, had been a conscientious objector in the second World War until the fall of Paris when, immediately, he joined up in a branch of intelligence and left for Cairo.

Soon it was time for lunch. Morning duties were always light as Percy rose late.

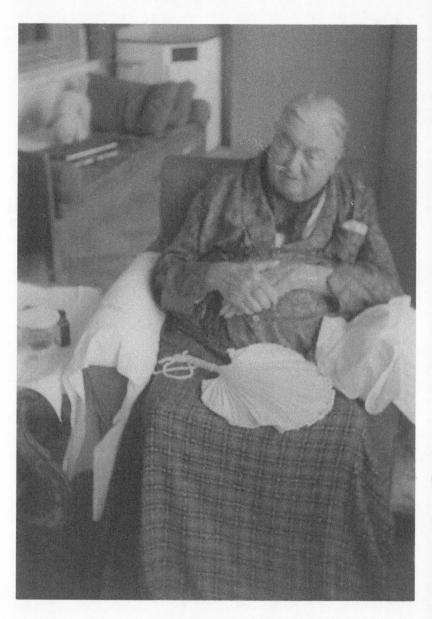

Percy Lubbock at Gli Scafari

6

Hugh joined us on the loggia for lunch. *Oeuf Florentine* and meringues. He had been working hard and was pleased to find John cheerful in my company – even if Percy hadn't caught our mood. Hugh suggested that I try a little reading aloud in the afternoon. 'We will select something for you and will be near at hand if any difficulties arise.' I began to feel more at home with him. He had clever, humorous and kind eyes. I liked his way of expressing himself too. It was a bit antiquated; almost Shakespearian. He spoke of Milan (pronouncing it Millern) and Marseilles (accent on last syllable and emphasising the l's and the s's) as he, unconsciously, began to teach me local history. John liked a 'tuck in' and Percy didn't speak but became, possibly, a little resigned to my presence.

I did read to Percy that afternoon but the boys steered the

choice, suggesting I took up where Hugh had left off – towards the end of *Martin Chuzzlewit*. Not easy to read aloud but it seemed to go all right until, with a jerk of the hand, Percy stayed me. I was reading the words 'If friars bear such hearts as thine, Tom, let friars multiply..' when he expostulated. 'Dickens, although magnificent, could be horribly sentimental.' He loathed any mention of Tom Pinch.

I think we changed to *The Murder of Roger Ackroyd* by Agatha Christie 'I enjoy her little twists at the end', he said, 'and liked her very much. In the old days of course.'

The three of us got down to it again that evening – after Percy's bed time.

'We', Hugh said 'have found a drawer full of papers written by him about his horrifying wife. He was totally taken in by, and besotted with, her. 'Well.' John often started a sentence with that word. 'She was a fiend. Percy describes, with admiration, how every morning in summer she used to be transported in a Sedan chair to the bay. There she would be tipped into the water where she swam away like a fish.'

'Yes', Hugh took over. 'After being carried back she took to her bed and stayed there until Percy went in with his pencil torch and started to go blind.' Stories tumbled out and I was transfixed.

Maybe they needed one more person to enjoy their tantalising tales. Maybe they were desperate for me to be accepted there. But, as it turned out, we were becoming friends for life.

Later, when I pondered on it – as I often did, I think that what they lacked in their busy, conscientious, serious lives was a pet. Perhaps I stood in for a puppy or a kitten.

'Bed time', Hugh reminded, 'but more tomorrow.'

7

One morning, soon after my arrival, when Elena had settled me
with my breakfast tray, there was a knock on the door. I jumped out
of bed and pulled on my dressing gown. Hugh stood on the
landing. He didn't come in but handed me a small, portable
wireless, saying, 'we, as you probably guessed, share a room and
need only one of these. We thought our spare one might be of
comfort to you.' I think Hugh wanted me to know how things
stood. How shared their life was. Maybe he was fearful that I was
falling for John who had a tactile side; liked to stroke my arm and
finger my ear rings. Half puppy – half kitten.

Things fell into place. Those days, very hot and happy days,
began to roll into one. With John and Hugh – and, indeed, with
Percy, I was in good company – the very best. Although I was fond

of friends in England I found myself unable to miss them. Courtships, weddings, even births were going on amongst my contemporaries but it failed to bother me or bring pangs. I took over all John and Hugh's tasks and Percy was reconciled – even to the extent of becoming attached to me. Some mornings, when there were no letters to write or new periodicals to read, Percy enjoyed talking. He described himself as a radical and a humanist – was violently opposed to hunting or shooting as sports. He did not worry that the socialists might do away with Eton (the school about which he had written an elegant book *Shades of Eton*): 'My theory on why Eton and the other public schools started to grow is because middle-class parents couldn't think of what to do with their sons during the winter hunting season. What about that place Eton where the poor boys go? – they said. Let's pack them off there.'

Sometimes he would pat his huge stomach and say, 'Susanna. Let me tell you something. People, when they get old, either blow up or they dry up. I've blown up. Just wait and see what happens to you.'

Percy also liked to reminisce – speaking dreamily with his blind eyes closed and waiving his long and swollen fingers in the air as he told me, with reverence, of his admiration for the Danish ballet dancer, Adeline Genée. He had, as a very young man, hero-worshipped her. 'So light on her feet. So light. Like a tiny piece of fluff.' At some point he had obviously tracked her down and forged a friendship. 'On the table. The table next to the sofa, you will find a beautiful little box she gave me.' I did find it in the place that Percy had described. It was, indeed, beautiful. Green marble lined in blue velvet. Percy insisted on giving it to me. He had decided that

I looked like Adeline Genée. Here his imagination had strayed far. I was not exactly fat but on the chubby side and certainly didn't float about like a piece of fluff. I still treasure the box.

John and Hugh were able to go away together for the day – sometimes for a night or two. In Florence they much enjoyed telling Nicky Mariano (Bernard Berenson's companion in life) how Percy had 'fallen for a pretty young lady.' Letters of teasing interest began to arrive and I had to answer them.

Percy dictated 'Yes. I am lucky to have Susanna. She has promised to stay with me for ever.' I didn't want to write that. Not to admit on paper that I was to live forever with an old, blind man in a marble palace overlooking the sea. John and Hugh were preparing for the next stage in their lives.

'Percy', I shouted (he was very deaf) 'Not forever. That was never agreed.'

'Well. Say for a very long time.' That matter over we turned to the flimsy air mail edition of *The Times*. He always kicked off with a joke. 'Any rash engagements?', then, 'any interesting deaths?'

Occasionally Percy reproached me for, in his pedantic view, my mispronunciation. Once I read out a snippet from the paper 'schizophrenic girl attacks Eros.' His clean hand shot up. 'Two' he said 'Two mistakes.' I had given both words, schizophrenic and Eros, the wrong emphasis. Nonetheless, I was very soon forgiven.

Sometimes, before taking his first morning sip or two, Percy appeared puzzled. Pointing to his innards he often asked 'Why am I me? Can you answer that? I can almost understand – but not quite – why you are you. But why me? Why am I me?' I was never able to comfort him on that topic.

I told him I wanted to visit Byron's Grotto. He chuckled and said, 'I always make my visitors take the trip there, just for amusement. Byron never swam anywhere near that place. When they get there I tell them to write "bosh" all over the walls. I call it Bosh Grotto.'

During my overlap with John and Hugh, Iris Origo (owner, of course, of the villa and custodian of Percy's welfare for his life) visited us – twice I think. Percy was always disappointed that her visits were rare and short although she frightened him into silence. She was a formidable creature with a gigantic brain and expensive clothes. Hugh did a wonderful imitation of her and the way she treated us – graciously as she might have done invaluable servants whose notice she wished to avert. In my case she praised my inner resource and increased my pocket money.

Not long after Iris's last visit. Percy's crabbed old lawyer, Bernadini, came all the way from Florence in a hired car with a driver. John and Hugh expected him and told me that he was 'rather a dear,' but that he hated dealing with Percy. Bernadini had been tipped off by Iris after she had witnessed the state of financial chaos and extravagance during her last visit to the Villa. John told me that he had been there on the occasion of a previous encounter when the lawyer had warned Percy that funds were running low. He had asked if three gardeners were really necessary with, 'How shall I put it? the *padrone* chair bound and unable to enjoy the sights out there. Wouldn't one lad be sufficient? Then there is the indoor staff. Alfredo and Maria, Elena as well as Dante doing odd jobs. Couldn't Elena and Dante manage on their own?'

Hugh told me that letters from the lawyer had remained unanswered. 'Some other time', Percy always said as one or other of the boys dealt with correspondence.

Percy, who lived in dread of Bernadini's visits, ordered stuffed eggs and said that lunch must be on the dot of one o'clock. John and Hugh both showed him to Percy's study where I sat reading aloud. Percy signalled that we were all to stay with him during the session. The nervy old lawyer steeled himself and refused to sit – but went close to his unwilling client and said, 'There is no money left. It has run out.'

'Run out? No. No. I felt sure there was enough for another fortnight.'

Eyes to heaven, Bernadini said, 'Your situation is unusual. Your step-daughter, as you know, owns the house and land and your wife left you a sum of money that was intended to support you. That is the sum that has run out. Your step-daughter is prepared to see to your comfort herself from now on but what we are querying is the rate at which you live. Here there is a valuable property in which you have a life interest.' So it was – acres of sea-front, olives and vines.

On he struggled 'One building – one only – perhaps one of the lodges – could be sold off for a large sum. Large enough to save the day.'

'If you say so. Perhaps we must. My wife would never have allowed it. My step-daughter must be consulted.'

'She has agreed to it *Signor*. All she wants from you is a signature.'

Hugh guided Percy's puffy hand over a document prepared in advance by Bernadini – as Percy's blank eyes turned towards the urn on the mantelpiece. We all ate our stuffed eggs in semi-silence and the miserable old man scurried away as soon as he dared. None of us, as far as I can remember, ever learnt whether the lodge was sold or not.

41

After one of John and Hugh's absences and after Mahler in the evening, John said, 'I don't think we have yet told you about Henry James's letters. Mercy.' Hugh said 'Yes. We found a stack of letters to Percy from Henry James. They all begin *'Carissimo Ragazzo'*

John chuckled, 'Great Scott. Imagine Percy ever being a *ragazzo* – let alone a *carissimo* one.'

Hugh always carried a large, flat white box of Sullivan and Powell cigarettes and smoked them non-stop. He must have brought supplies from London. He enlarged on the subject of Percy's connection with Henry James – saying, 'The thing about never violating a character's point of view is normally attributed to Henry James but, in fact, the rule seems to have been formulated by Percy himself.'

John urged Hugh to stand up and to recite me one of the letters. It seemed he had learnt several by heart. 'Very well then', he said, 'Just for Zanna.'

He was an excellent mimic and spoke very clearly. At first he pretended to be Percy – holding a wine glass in his hand.

'Dear Henry was on a visit to New York. I remember it well. In that letter he told me that he had been entertained, I think, at the Century Club, by a group of young people. He became aware that, at the end of the room, there was an easel that held a painting under a sheet. Poor Henry. He realised that they were going to present him with it.'

Hugh put down the glass and re-entered as Henry James.

'It was unveiled and revealed a nudity of the most pronounced variety. What could I do? I couldn't leave it behind for fear of offending the young people. Had I taken it home, my housekeeper (Mrs Paddington) would see that her worst fears were justified.

42

She'd realise that my reasons for this trip to America were dissolute ones.'

John and I were near to collapsing. John asked me, 'Has he shown you Henry James's watch yet?'

'No. What a swizz.'

'Henry gave it to Percy on his twenty-fourth birthday and said, 'If you knew how cruel you were to be twenty four – you wouldn't be it. You wouldn't be it.'

Hugh said that Percy was sure to bring out the watch before long and that it was time for bed.

John wouldn't have that and fetched us each another glass of disgusting wine as he continued to give me advice.

He thought that, when conversation with Percy got sticky, I should try talking about Virginia Woolf. She had veered between praising and castigating Percy as a writer. In her 1923 diaries she accused him of pedantic insincerity in his ground-breaking analysis of the novel – *The Craft of Fiction*. I tried that the next day and his blind eyes rolled. 'Women. Oh dear. Women. I did not admire her in the least.'

On the other hand both John and Hugh said it would be fatal to mention either Somerset Maugham or Geoffrey Scott. Somerset Maugham had immortalised Percy's wife, Lady Sybil, in a short story called 'Louise'. He had asked for trouble when, in the tale, he called Louise's daughter Iris. It told of a hypochondriac whose fancied illnesses dominated the lives of her family. When Iris tried to break away Louise reproachfully died. Maugham had made it very clear who he had in mind. His name was not allowed to be uttered in Percy's hearing – nor were there any copies of his books in the house.

Geoffrey Scott had more or less thrown Sybil out – so his name, too, was a dirty word. Nonetheless we did find a copy of *The Architecture of Humanism* in one of Percy's shelves. None of us could imagine how it came to be there. It was not an early edition and this particular copy had a printed letter on the inside, 'I have read your book thirteen times and find it tiresome.'

Hugh looked cheerful so I pressed on with my enquiries.

'What about Edith Wharton?'

'Well, of course, Percy and Edith fell out when he married Sybil. He had been Edith's slave until then.'

John said, 'Percy was an epicene character; frightfully wet in those days. Once he and Edith were on a boulevard together in Paris. She had five little dogs on separate leads that gathered up onto one handle.'

'Yes', Hugh added, 'she gave the handle to Percy and told him to hold it for a moment. Well. She disappeared to have her hair done – leaving him in charge of the dogs for three hours. Poor Percy. He had never cared for dogs.'

Finally Hugh got his way and we all went to bed.

8

Emboldened by my hours with John and Hugh, I took my place next to Percy and our props and said, 'the boys tell me that Henry James was a great friend of yours.'

'I'm proud of that' he said 'maybe I was a sort of protégé of his. So very much younger.' Out came the watch and the story of Percy's twenty-fourth birthday. 'You wouldn't be it. You wouldn't be it' – told to me twice.

I pressed on. 'Please Percy. Tell me more of him.'

He sipped, glanced at the ashes and, with amusement, reminisced. 'I well remember dear Henry being introduced to a bevy of beauties. Amongst them was the celebrated actress, Ellen Terry. I asked him what he had made of them and he replied "one of the miserable wantons was not without a certain cadaverous charm" – dear Henry. A long time ago. Henry, though, could have a harsh side. I well remember how he discouraged our friend, Howard Sturgis, from writing another novel after the publication of *Belchamber* in 1904. Henry said it was unsatisfactory. Poor Howard. He went on to write only one more short story about a lesser writer driven to suicide by the criticism of a greater one. Edith Wharton praised the book – but it was Henry's approval that Howard wanted. 'I'd like you to read *Belchamber* and give me your view.' I read it and, unlike Henry James, found it very satisfactory.

Since John and Hugh had suggested that I talk to Percy of his wife and also of his own works – I had a crack at both – with equal success.

Percy told me that he was a communist and that, all things considered, a coffee-coloured baby was a delightful thing. Unfortunately, though, Thomas Hardy wrote badly. That amazed me.

Referring to his own works he chuckled, 'Balzac. Do you know what I once wrote about Balzac?'

'No Percy. I fear I don't'

'Balzac was great but his taste was abominable. I actually said that in print.' He sighed and added 'all we writers asked for in those days were copious draughts of unqualified praise.'

Little did we know what John and Hugh were heading for in the way of copious draughts. None of us did – least of all John and Hugh.

The boys took me for drives in that dramatic part of the world and the days were blissful until there came a stir in the air as they plotted their departure. They were happy that Percy had taken to me – almost to their exclusion. After our three months under the same glorious roof (a long time for erstwhile strangers to share a home) the dreadful day of their leaving for Asolo arrived. Folders, typewriters and leather luggage were stuffed into the black Fiat. Elena and I cried beside great lemon pots – the lemons seemed to be crying too. John and Hugh both embraced me – vowing to return before long. Hugh said, 'and of course you are to keep the wireless.' I'd forgotten that it wasn't mine.

Things changed that day but not one drop of our friendship ever ran out. Not until Hugh died on May 20th 2016 – aged eighty eight. For many years I had been a puppy no more – by then I was an eighty-year-old multiple grandmother.

9

I was alone with Percy and did become a tinge melancholy. Apart from the staggering beauty of the place – there was little to distract me and much of the reading was beyond my power to appreciate. I liked Percy though, and reading aloud, even when out of my depth, amused me. Percy was a disciple of Walter Pater and called upon me to halt from time to time as I read from his slow-moving works. 'Take account of him my dear. "To burn always with this hard gem-like flame to maintain this ecstasy is success in life" – not always easy but advice worth following. Pater also told us to "getting as many pulsations as possible into the given time."'

Percy, slumped – fairly drunk – in his chair, didn't look as though he had ever experienced a single pulsation or, indeed, any moment of ecstasy. Nor did I pulsate much at that time. I always dreaded reading Henry James aloud. Percy who had, more than once, been described as 'more Jamesian than James' was entirely familiar with all his novels and often allowed me to choose which one to read to him. Sometimes he would halt me, pain on his face, and say 'Oh dear. That was a bad bit of Henry. Not his best at all. Dear Henry. Of course it was a very early work.' I was reading from *The Princess Casamassima*. Maybe the plot was too violently political for Percy. He certainly considered Hyacinth Robinson too flawed a character to be a suitable hero.

A big compensation at that time was meeting Nina Lucas, a refreshing and warm-hearted widow who, with two pretty teenage daughters, sometimes stayed in a house nearby. We became close friends until she died many years later.

John and Hugh telephoned most nights. Having lived at Gli Scafari for four years they always wanted to know how things were going there. They sounded happy and excited. They had, at last, settled down to an independent life and stimulating work poured in.

True, as always, to their word, they came to visit regularly. Things had slightly changed between us. I was no longer their protégé – but in full charge of housekeeping and Percy was semi-besotted with me. But our compatibility had equalised and became even closer than before. Their life, however, was opening up while mine seemed to be shutting down a bit – although many fascinating things went on at Gli Scafari. Percy's old hangers-on still visited – but their turns were as nothing compared to the arrival of John and Hugh.

Among those who considered Gli Scafari a necessary part of an Italian tour, were Hugh and Alexandra Trevor Roper. Hugh Trevor

Roper (later Lord Dacre) was by then a well known historian – his chief interests being England in the sixteenth and seventeenth century – and Nazi Germany. His wife, Lady Alexandra, was a tall, wan beauty. Their visit was a huge flop. Neither of them wanted to talk to me but pressed for uninterrupted access to Percy. Percy resented that since he liked me to be involved in all conversation. 'Poor manners,' he said. Then Trevor Roper failed to get the measure of Percy when he suggested taking over my morning tasks. He picked out a few unsuitable snatches from *The Times* (rape and murder) to read aloud. Percy was horrified and swore never to let them set foot in the house again. Later, in 1983, Trevor Roper's reputation was much damaged when he attributed verification to the Hitler diaries – shown shortly afterwards to be forgeries. Percy would have chortled.

Derek Hill came several times but spent most of his visits blocking the only telephone line as he planned his next social escapades. He was already established as a painter and lived in Rome where he was a director of the Fine Arts Society at the British School. I had never met anyone remotely like him. Half the time he was merry and the other half he was cross. He seemed, to me, to be resentful of the role I played at Gli Scafari. Not that I had met him before or was even certain as to what role I did play. One evening he shouted, 'Everyone thinks it's pretty far-fetched – the way you are so at home with Percy. I've known him MUCH longer than you have.' I couldn't make head or tail of him and Percy didn't care for him at all. 'Terribly selfish I'm afraid. We won't have him again', he said as he chuckled with delight when Derek left. I didn't wholly agree with Percy. There was something endearing about Derek. He showed flashes of affection and pressed me to stay with him in Ireland if ever I got the opportunity. The night he left, John, with amusement, told me on the telephone how he and Hugh had once been late in keeping a date with Derek at the British School. They had found a note awaiting them there – pinned to the door. It read, 'Good night and good bye. D. Hill.' Derek was always searching for slights. On one occasion he brought with him a Pop artist who was also living in Rome. His name was Joe Tilson. Percy was tickled and called him 'Pop' throughout the evening.

Willy Mostyn-Owen, a protégé of Berenson's, also appeared in a huge and dashing car. He was staying, as a student, at I Tatti and Percy always liked gossip from Florence. I, too, enjoyed his visits as he took me for drives in the dashing car.

Once John and Hugh came for several nights. I think it was in the autumn. It was wonderful of them as they had an increasing amount of work but they worried about my isolation. They brought their typewriters with them. Hugh was busily researching his guide book to Venice. Their independent life at Asolo amused them – seeing much of Freya Stark (in whose garden they lived) and Marina Luling at Maser – and being easily able to get to Venice. John loved the release from constant Mahler and began to build up his (eventually vast) collection of recordings. He understood music to an unusual extent. They were happy to have set up a home together, 'but', Hugh said, 'one day our plan is to buy something near Lucca in Tuscany. There is a magnificent carved, wooden figure of Christ in the cathedral there.' That was the first time I had ever heard of Lucca. He went on to say, 'from there we could be involved in the libraries of Florence and I very much hope to create a garden.' Hugh always, and emphatically, pronounced the letters 'ol' as in the word mole. I have never heard anyone else do that. It represented one of his many delightful quirks. 'SOLved, invOLved, dissOLved.'

John told me more of the wonders of the city of Lucca and of the glorious country surrounding it.

In the afternoon of one of their visits, the telephone rang and Hugh, who was downstairs, answered it in the hall. He came up to tell Percy, as John and I sat with him, that a certain Arthur Hobhouse had rung and asked if two of them could join us for lunch the next day. Percy pondered. 'Arthur Hobhouse. He's a terrible bore but I like her – Konradin. She once gave me an alarm clock. Tell them to come to lunch tomorrow.' Unusual for Percy to prefer a wife to a husband. 'Arthur is a very limited man' he went on 'but Konradin' – turning to me 'you will enjoy Konradin.'

I was sent to greet them at the front door and John came with me. The guests arrived on time at a quarter to one. Arthur Hobhouse, dapper in summer Sunday white, came forward. He had a moustache. He said 'may I introduce you to my companion. Miss Lewis.' Miss Lewis was many years younger than her protector and very dressy. John touched my arm and said, 'Good Grief' or it may have been 'mercy.'

The alarm clock given to Percy by Konradin was wound up and ticking. Elena had scuttled about in Percy's bedroom until she discovered its hiding place. She set it correctly, squinting through slits, and placed it beside the Elba wine and salted almonds. Percy threw up his hands. 'My dears. Konradin – I draw attention to a priceless object. It is always here – ticking by my side. As you know – I cannot see, so the pleasure of hearing it tick is a heightened one. Come closer.'

Hugh went to him 'Percy. Mr Hobhouse is here with Miss Lewis. I don't think you have met her before.'

'What's that? Not Konradin? Oh dear me no. That won't do at all.' Poor Hugh with his exquisite manners was confused and held back. 'Tell him to come some other time,' Percy insisted.

Miss Lewis looked aghast. It had been her idea. She had put pressure on her elderly lover to introduce her to the man of letters. The lover was unmanned, knock-kneed; wished he hadn't boasted about his acquaintances. He advanced as John and I did our best to hide our amusement. 'Percy. Miss Lewis is an admirer of your work.'

Percy gave in with no grace and speeded up the arrival of lunch. It was, as usual, served on the loggia that opened out of Percy's sitting room. Alfredo, white coated and gloved, carried the egg-dominated food from the bowels of the house (as he had done since Percy became restricted to living upstairs). That was one of the cook's many bugbears. Soufflés flopped as they travelled from the kitchen. John and Hugh did their best to entertain Arthur and Miss Lewis as I tried to soothe Percy. Not long after lunch the guests departed with minimum farewells and 'another time bring Konradin' as parting shot.

Percy was grumpy for the rest of the day but John, Hugh and I delighted in re-running the drama until late that night. The alarm clock was soon put away again. Percy said that the ticking of it aggravated him.

10

By the spring I needed a break. Friends from England wrote to say it was time I went home. My mother was unwell and my parents were moving house. With much help from John and Hugh we found a temporary replacement. A nice young man with a beard. Percy was furious and refused to like the poor boy – but off I went; promising to return when a month or so was over. Very soon after getting back to England, I met Nicholas Johnston, an architect who had been at Cambridge with Hugh Honour. We had both found the very thing that John and Hugh recognised in each other. The perfect companion. Nicky and I soon decided to marry and were very happy – but there were snags. My promise to return to Lerici and my relationship with John and Hugh. Although, of course, that was unbalanced since they had each other, we had become – almost

– an emotional trio – having often talked about adventures and holidays that we would one day share. I daresay I had expected that I was always to remain single. For me to plan to marry seemed like a slight betrayal. I wrote to them and explained what had happened and also to tell them that my next sojourn at Lerici was to be a short one. Very soon a letter came back. It was written by John on his Olivetti typewriter.

'We've been thinking of nothing else. Hugh says that, as long as it's Nicky Johnston, that's all right.' Hugh, from their Cambridge days, knew Nicky to be clever, civilised and likely to allow me to be free, sometimes, to spend time with them. John ended the letter by saying 'But, Great Scott, how are you going to break it to Percy? Hugh joins me in sending his fondest love.'

Nicky recently found in a box of old papers, an invitation sent out in the somewhat formal manner of the day. It said, 'Mr Hugh Honour at Home'. At the top was written, 'Mr Nicholas Johnston'.

The party, ten or twelve guests at the most – all male – took place in Hugh's panelled rooms at St Catherine's College.

Nicky remembers admiring a small renaissance drawing of a male nude, nicely framed and hanging on the wall.

Hugh said, 'That's by Annibale Caracci.' With Hugh's singularly emphatic diction, it sounded like Annie Barley Karachi.

With a pay-off from his time in the army, Hugh had already started to collect works of art. In those days he could well have found such a drawing on the bulging barrows of Soho for less than five pounds.

I wrote to Percy, too.

His reply, dictated to the bearded young man, reached me in London. 'My dear Susanna. This has come as a terrible shock. I arrive at a serious matter; that of your intention to marry. I hope you are entering this of your own accord – that you are exercising your own free will. You have, after all, been very happy here. Are you under any unreasonable pressure? You know the rules don't you? Twenty four of everything. No young lady in my day would have considered anything less. Starting with twenty-four handker-chiefs. I look forward to seeing you here as soon as possible and I, for one, believe in very long engagements. I am keeping a brooch for you. It belonged to my wife.'

John and Hugh had often met Derek Hill at Lerici and, although he was entertaining and talented, they found his self-centredness and querulous character hard to handle. They could never resist teasing him and found the perfect opportunity.

During my 'break' from Lerici and after I had told Nicky I would happily marry him, I stood by a promise to go for a week to stay with Derek at his pretty old red brick rectory, St Columbs, near Churchill in Donegal. He always made much of his colourful neighbour – Henry McIlhenny. He was a rich American philan-thropist, wit and legendary chairman of the Philadelphia Art Museum. For part of the year he lived at Glenveagh Castle – very near Derek. He was also a friend of John and Hugh's.

Derek played a sort of Mr Collins at the gate of Rosings.

'I MAY be able to get you included in a dinner party at Glenveagh' he said, very emphatically, on the day – if not the hour – of my arrival at St Columbs. John and Hugh knew of my visit there and knew, too, of the reverence in which Derek held Henry McIlhenny. 'Henry is very particular about who he invites', Derek went on, 'for instance Charlie Chaplin and Greta Garbo have both stayed there. I MIGHT have to leave you here alone. Gracie (his

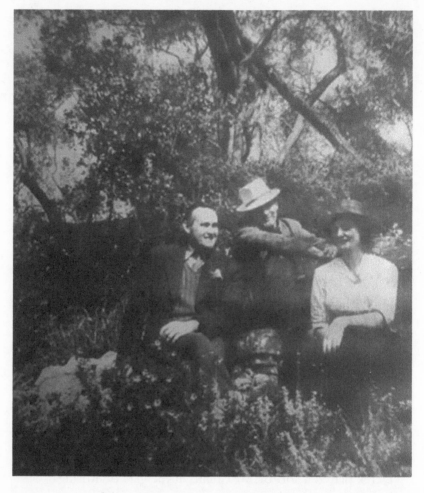

Derek Hill, Christopher McLaren and Susanna at St Columbs, Donegal, 1958

cook) would look after you. She makes wonderful bacon butties. I can't promise but I'll try. I won't ring him today because I know he has important visitors.'

As Derek ranted on about the difficulty of getting me an invitation to Glenveagh – there was a loud noise outside.

Henry McIlhenny had come himself with some of his 'important' visitors. He shouted 'Where is she? I want to meet Susanna. John and Hugh have just rung from Italy to say she's staying here. They say I've GOT to meet her. Bring her to dinner, of course, tomorrow.'

Derek was very much put out, not only by John and Hugh's role in the affair but also by the fact that I didn't marry a young man he had produced for me. The idea of our marriage had never occurred to either the young man or me; particularly as I was going to marry Nicky. Derek said, pouting, 'I asked him specially and took a lot of trouble to get you both here at the same time. There's gratitude.' I was forgiven, though, and Derek sent me a very slinky frock made entirely from black beads as a wedding present. He had found it in an antique shop in Dublin.

After my rather extended 'month off' – during which time I had become engaged to Nicky – I was bound to return to Gli Scafari and to stay there until I had found a more permanent replacement than that of the short-term bearded boy. John and Hugh arranged to overlap with me there. I knew they would be helpful in softening Percy up and convincing him that Nicky was not Bluebeard and that I was not under unreasonable pressure.

Nicky had planned to join us there for a week. Before he arrived, Percy was grumpy and said 'Oh dear. I thought you were happy here' – over and over again. Hugh was staunch and repeatedly told him 'Percy. Nicky Johnston is an old friend of mine. You will like him very much.'

Nicky did join us and Percy found it difficult to fault him. He gave in with some grace and fumbled blindly in a box that he always kept near to where he sat. From it he extracted a gigantic

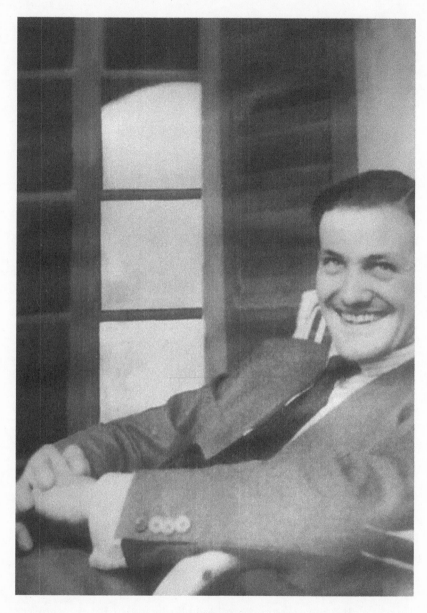

Nicky at Gli Scafari

aquamarine – set in platinum. 'I wish' he said, 'I wish I were able to give you twenty four of these. It belonged to my wife.'

I was pleased to own Lady Sibyl's beautiful brooch. Heaven knows how the news of Percy's present spread so fast but, within days, one of Percy's nieces wrote to me saying 'We have ALL decided that you deserve the brooch.' Hugh was amused and said, 'it must have been something the whole family has been discussing at length.'

We found a replacement reader of sorts and I went back to England to marry Nicky on December 4th 1958.

11

Of course things changed. John and Hugh could not come to our wedding in December 1958 but sent a beautiful pair of cloudy, white, glass candle-sticks from Venice – along with messages of love. We stayed in close touch and sometime in about 1962, John told me by telephone the exciting news that they had found a perfect house in the Lucchesia and were ready to buy it and move there. They asked me to fly to Pisa to spend a few nights with them at the Universo Hotel in Lucca and to rejoice with them. I was busy having babies but took leave of them and Nicky to join the boys.

They met me in the black Fiat at Pisa airport and we went straight to the Universo Hotel. It stood on the corner of the Piazza Napoleone and the Piazza del Teatro. The Piazza Napoleone was then used as a massive car park that heaved and honked with

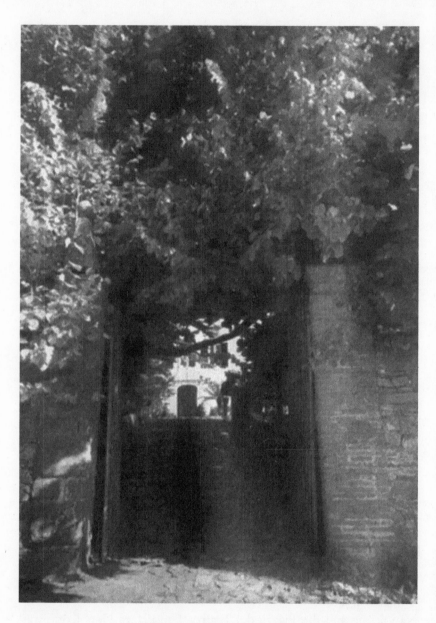

Gated entrance to Villa Marchio

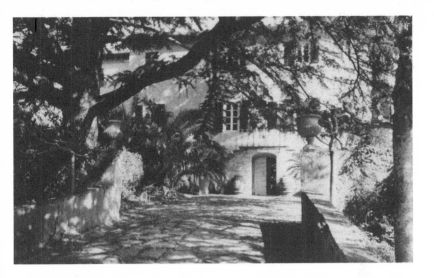

Front of Villa Marchio

motors. Hugh was able to leave the car there. Even then the hotel was faded – battered and stately; old fashioned with well dressed attendants. It was comfortable – not exactly run down but dark, dusty and very central.

The first evening we walked in Lucca – John and Hugh showing me the city's eccentricities as well as its beauties. Hugh always smoking and John trailing a little behind. At supper we talked exclusively of the property they had bought and how, the next day, I was to be shown it. Both John and Hugh had some furniture stored away in England and, together, from Asolo, they had been spotting and buying treasures that they had been able to keep in one of Freya Stark's barns.

In the morning we took the old road from Lucca to Florence and, after about ten kilometres, turned to the left towards the mountains. Then we wound up, Hugh honking on the horn all the

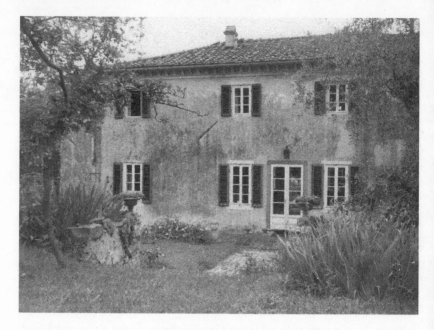

Back of Villa Marchio

way, through one or two tiny villages where old ladies in black sat outside on rickety chairs. After a bit we came to an interesting old house with a chapel attached to it and overhung with dark trees where we turned right and right again. Then on to a rough track rolling gently down hill towards a group of buildings half hidden by trees. We could see an enclosing wall, roofs, the shadow of a giant cedar and, beyond it, a wide view of the valley stretching across the plain to the Pisan hills. It might have been the background of a fifteenth century Madonna.

Hugh parked the car, we rounded a wall and came to a gate. We pushed it open and walked up a steep paved path to the house. This was the Villa Marchio which, on account of the obscuring trees, only began to emerge in my eyes as we got nearer. It was painted

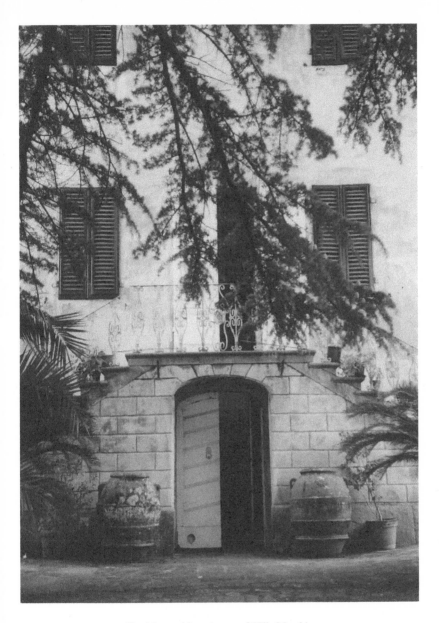

Double outside staircase of Villa Marchio

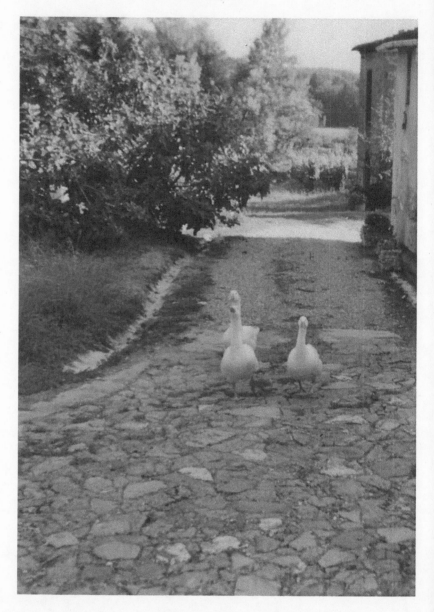

The geese at Villa Marchio

in a blotchy and peeling pink. A double flight of stairs led up to the front door. On each side of the house there was a set-back wing. John and Hugh were already the owners and had been given a big, rusty key with which to let ourselves in. In front of us was a wide hall – two windows and a glass door at the back. From there we looked to a garden that tilted up behind the house and beyond which rose the mountains. Tortoises crawled everywhere in the wild undergrowth. There was a big room on the right of the hall with a smaller one beyond. Perfection. All they could ever need – and way beyond.

Set into one of the garden walls was a tiny chapel which we later explored. John and Hugh had not had the chance to do that before. They had had to make up their minds to buy the property at great speed. Vendors had been impatient. The chapel was still consecrated and showed traces of sanctity; fragments of candle sticks, a crucifix with broken arms, wet altar cloths. Two collapsed pews – a cobwebbed wine bottle covering one. Hugh took it all very calmly but with obvious delight. John's eyes sparkled in utter joy.

After they moved to Tofori John and Hugh did, in the early sixties, visit a declining Percy at Lerici more than once and found it dreadfully sad. Percy's nephew and his wife, Georgette (who Hugh called Flannelette), had moved in and taken charge. According to Hugh she had served lunch in a bathing dress. No sign of Alfredo or Maria. The house was a mess and Percy, to their mind, was ill-cared for and unhappy. To make things worse there was a huge caravan parked permanently in the drive. It was inhabited by Georgette's hatchet-faced sister, her poet (not published) husband and two messy daughters. We were all particularly sad, though, when we were given further evidence of the decline. My brother, Alexander Chancellor, worked in Milan and spent a weekend with friends near Forte del Marmi. From there he drove over to see Percy. He wrote to me afterwards and I forwarded the letter to John and Hugh.

I quote from Alexander's letter:

'I was greeted, conspiratorially, at the kitchen door by your squinty friend (is she called Elena?) and smuggled upstairs where she tried to make me drink a martini. We talked about you and your babies and Nicky and the late Pope – and then about Percy, whom she secretly arranged for me to visit. I went into his room to find everything exactly the same. There was Percy looking vast in an arm chair. He asked very tenderly about you. "It has been pointed out to me", he said, "that I have just come of age for the fourth time. I think that Susanna should come and see me very soon as I doubt if I have long to live." (That may be true as, apparently, he is always nearly dying.) "Tell Susanna that I think about her very much." He finished "I thought I ought to tell you that anyway." Apparently her taking me to see Percy was Elena's last act of defiance. Georgette, who appeared afterwards in a furious temper reminded her of a much repeated rule that she should never take people to see Percy without first applying to her. Later I learnt that Elena had been sacked and is soon to leave. Georgette took me downstairs. In the hall a niece of hers was playing ping-pong with a hairy *'meridionale'* boyfriend. The drawing room was looking very denuded and dingy and there was only Cinzano to drink. They obviously have a bad time financially and Georgette, with her austerity programme, is finally supreme. She says she is now happier there as she has discovered nice friends in La Spezia and has a full social life. Also that Percy doesn't drink any more.'

The boys were horrified when they read my brother's letter but Hugh said, 'at least Flannelette didn't wear a bathing dress.'

We moved house in London and, slightly to John and Hugh's disappointment (which was not to last) had four daughters. From this time on my memories of our friendship will be recorded in shreds and snatches. London, Lucca – a trip to Holland. Many letters (mostly lost thanks to faded faxes) and constant contact. We did, once or twice, manage to stay with them early on in their lives at Tofori. Their literary output was increasing and their industry was astounding. At that early stage they employed a couple – Gilda, noisy, bossy and with long red finger nails, cooked and her husband Andrea helped in the garden as it began to flourish. Hugh was never easy in the role of employer and Gilda terrified him. We weren't allowed to be a second late for meals. John took things more in his stride. Together they created a lotus pond and Nicky helped them with sketches for a loggia. Below the house were clusters of barns and cottages. Cackling geese, croaking frogs and ticking cicadas created a world of wonder.

In London they did occasionally stay with us but it wasn't ideal. Four children, school runs, chaotic breakfasts and scatty au pair girls. Nicky was hard at work in the basement of the house where he had set up his first private practice. Usually the boys went to their friend, Patrick Kinross, a writer known for his work on Islamic history, in his large house in Maida Vale. They were a little uneasy in London – particularly Hugh, who was shy by nature. He was always very smartly and formally dressed when there. He had enough suits to last him a life time (his figure never altered) and always wore a waistcoat. His shirts were sent to him by Bays of

71

Cambridge and tended towards discreet checks; possibly very narrow pin stripes. John (strictly only when in London) wore a dark suit with a waistcoat and watch chain. As well as visiting museums, publishers, lawyers and friends, they had appointments with doctors and dentists. I well remember, after one of these sessions, John saying 'Well. Our dentist is very pleased with our teeth.' Can there ever have been such togetherness?

Neither of them liked parties or big dinners but they did, sometimes, go to them. They were, to their bewilderment, beginning to be lionised.

On one of their visits I drove them to Northamptonshire to see my uncle, Robin Chancellor, who lived in one of a pair of pavilions that were joined by curving colonnades. The main house had long since been destroyed by fire but the remaining pavilions are generally thought to be rare survivals of work by Inigo Jones.

I still have the letter John wrote to me after that.

'It was *terribly* kind of you to take us to Stoke Park. We *very* much enjoyed it. Could you forward on or give the enclosed to your uncle Robin? I don't know his address and want to ask him if he could give a nice photograph of the pavilions for reproduction in a book on Inigo Jones which Summerson has written for a Penguin series we are editing. Hugh has been arguing with me – saying that one ought not to address your uncle as Robin on so brief an acquaintance! If you think I shouldn't be so familiar, please *don't* forward the enclosed! Hugh is getting very stuffy about such things – or perhaps it is just living amongst formal Italians who always shake hands whenever you meet them. It was a shame that you had to go away. The rest of our visit was mostly work and rather a rush. We had dinner one night with Willy and Gaia [Mostyn-Owen]. *Pity* you

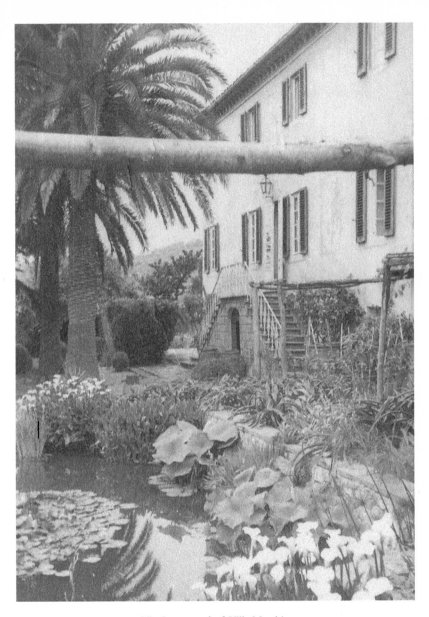

The lotus pond of Villa Marchio

missed it. There were the Annans and the C. P Snows. Tom Balogh, Nubar Gulbenkian and the Agnellis! Such a shame you weren't there. Neither of us enjoyed it much. David Carritt is on top of the world after the Rembrandt sale – Christie's certainly are edging up on Sotheby's. A friend of David's told us that he had already been offered a directorship and had refused because he couldn't face the prospect of having to conduct a sale! I suppose it must be true – though I had never thought of David as bashful.

We are busy gardening – it really *will* look rather exotic this summer with all the curious plants we have been collecting. You *must* come again soon. Can't you persuade Nicky to forget the children and come here for your holiday? No more news from Lerici. Hugh and I will go over next week if there is a nice sunny day. So far the spring has been very mild but only odd days of clear sun and sky. But no complaints – the lotus has already begun to shoot. Hugh joins me in sending his fondest love.'

12

We had often all talked together about whether Nicky and I should try to buy a small house near Lucca. I would be able to take all the girls there for the entire summer holidays – Nicky joining us for some weeks at a time. Easter holidays too and spells in between. That way – we would always be in close touch with the boys; a part of their family. After much discussion I wrote to tell them that we had finally made up our minds to go ahead and search.

Another of the few letters from John that I managed to keep.

'July 1966

Great excitement! There is *nothing* Hugh and I would look forward to more than you and Nicky getting a house near here. It would be lovely for us. I shall do everything I possibly can to help. The house I think would be perfectly charming is the one very near

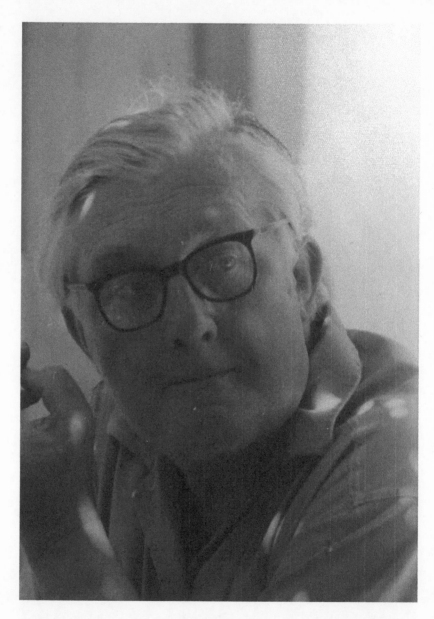

John

here. Despite his polite remarks when we were shown round, I don't think it appealed to Hugh. I don't understand why.'

Here I break to say that it occurred to me that the more cautious Hugh might have considered it too near to them – before long a house full of teenage girls and their noisy friends.

John continued. 'It is at present painted an unfortunate dead white all over and stands in a very bare patch. It would be much nicer if there were trees close to it, but of course that can quite easily be remedied as can the white of the exterior. I *strongly* recommend it. It could be lived in straightaway though obviously a purchaser would want to make alterations and improvements – about which more anon. It has electric light, is near a road and its own entry or drive would not cost much to put back in good condition. It has water from a large cistern. But the municipal water supply is close to the house and could easily be attached to it. About improvements; the house always appealed to us because it lends itself to a very attractive eventual enlargement – by building in between the house and the barn you would face in exactly the right direction – like here – South-West. Slightly more South than West. It really could I am *convinced* be made, in time, a most attractive place. Nor would it be prodigiously expensive. The price when I last enquired – several months ago – was £5000 – this includes the house, barn and several acres of olives and vines. It seems to be a bargain at present day prices. Perhaps you should stop having babies or even more enlargement might be needed!

There are, I am sure, several other possibilities – one very big indeed and the other an abandoned cottage – much less practical a possibility, I thought, to the one above. But, really, you and Nicky ought to come here for a few days and explore. I will make

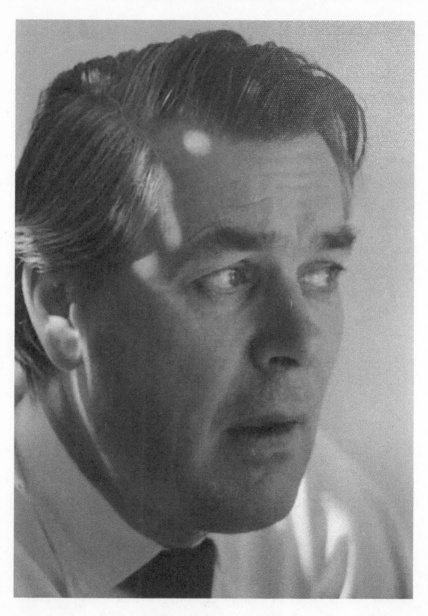

Hugh by Julian Alexander

enquiries beforehand and prepare things if you decide to come. You can fly to Pisa where we would meet you. Quite apart from Hugh and I having chosen this part of Tuscany – it is much more beautiful and liveable in than further south. The climate is much better – cooler in summer and much less cold in winter. Three cheers for the Lucchesia.

Do write very soon and let me know what you want me to do – both of us are entirely at your service. Hugh joins me in sending his fondest love.'

That clinched it. They wanted us to be near and we wanted to be near them for long spells during years to come.

13

During those exciting years, as we house-hunted in Tuscany and John and Hugh visited England, we saw a great deal of each other. In London, besides looking at works of art and making deals with publishers, they often indulged in a bit of light relief. Once they took me to a party of the stout and puffy Viva King – a famous *salonnière*. Her 'show' friend was then April Ashley who, according to Francis King, 'had emerged as a beautiful young butterfly from the drab chrysalis of a lanky merchant seaman.' John, on being introduced muttered 'good grief' but Hugh kept as far away from her as possible.

In Italy I often stayed with them at the villa. John used to wait, sometimes by the hour, leaning over the garden wall, spectacles gleaming through white wisteria, for my arrival. Usually he held a list in his hand for fear of forgetting things in need of discussion. 'Mercy. We have so much to catch up on.' Hugh had found living-in servants to be an anxiety and claustrophobic – so Gilda and Andrea were placed in a nearby cottage and Hugh took full charge of the cooking. He did it skilfully and enjoyed it, saying 'cooking is far easier than writing books' as he pored over Elizabeth David's recipes. He wrote books, too, of course, and created a magnificent garden. His eventual dream was to earn enough money so as to be able to write all morning and garden all afternoon. The house bulged, along with other treasures, with plant catalogues and gardening magazines.

The Villa had been transformed and was now a knock-out. The first floor hall which you came up to from the double flight of outdoor steps, was a striking room. Over the fireplace, embedded in the wall, was a fine marble low-relief of Edward 1st having the wounds sucked from his arm by Eleanor, his Queen. On the same wall there were two chunks of low shelves to take John and Hugh's folio collection and on the one opposite the fireplace was a long full-height book case flanked by a pair of silver, shell-shaped grotto chairs. Across the back of the room by the French window leading to the garden was an elegant regency sofa. Through the French window you now saw, in due season, tumbling Banksia roses instead of brambles.

As Hugh cooked supper, John and I were allowed to talk alone together. Hugh was not keen on this and, apart from pre-meal times (when it was impossible to avoid such a situation) solo talks were not permitted. John could be unwary and Hugh was often afraid he might let something slip out that he considered better not to. One evening, as we sipped and waited for our supper summons, John told me how his parents, living at Berwick on Tweed, had been forced to sell a part of their garden for a new, wider road. With the money from that they were able to send John to Rugby where he excelled himself in the art classes. A painting he did, sadly untraceable, won an international competition and was reproduced in the press. He wanted to be a painter and wrote to Stanley Spencer for advice. 'Well. He sent a nice letter but offered no help.' John's eyes had always been weak so he abandoned the idea of painting and trained to be a solicitor.

He also told me (which would certainly not have been allowed had Hugh been present and the telling of which stopped abruptly when supper was ready) of his long and tricky tracking down of Hugh and how he persuaded him to become his lifelong companion. John was eight years older than Hugh but would often return to Cambridge for parties given by 'queer' dons. Hugh was then a handsome and cautious undergraduate 'But, mercy, I won him over.'

He went on to say that Hugh's father, an electro-plater and silver smith in Tonbridge Wells, had gone bankrupt 'which is why Hugh is often anxious about spending – money frightens him but he is, as you know, also extremely generous.'

Supper, as always when Hugh cooked, was terrific. The boys both had original and unworldly reactions to almost everything. Once a local row had broken out and John said, 'Of course it's ESSENTIAL to take sides. Always back the person you like best – no matter who is in the wrong.' Distinctly the opposite to the view held by many who live in terror of falling out with anybody – often at the expense of loyalty. I was much reassured by John's attitude and realised that, were I to commit several murders, he would always take my part.

Their togetherness, as the years went by, seemed to become more and more pronounced. 'We don't care for them' – 'we haven't read that yet,' 'we didn't sleep very well last night.' To me it was utterly charming. I have never known two people, before or since, who lived together, worked together and did both in perfect harmony.

Nicky and I often went there for short breaks – in part to see our new house that was being renovated. It was called La Cavina and was small and shady; built into a hill and surrounded by an overgrown olive grove.

Once John and Hugh planned one of their favourite excursions for us. They wanted us to become familiar with the neighbourhood. Hugh packed a picnic lunch and we headed for Bagni di Lucca – a small town, high in chestnut woods to the North of Lucca and renowned, since Etruscan times, for its thermal springs.

Hugh drove. Nicky sat beside him and John and I gossiped in whispers at the back of the car. The road goes past the dramatic Ponte della Maddalena – a narrow mediaeval bridge, where we stopped. The bridge rears up at a perilous angle and crosses the river Serchio. We climbed, on foot, slowly to the apex where Hugh told us that it had originally been called the Ponte del Diavolo. A man, working there late one night, was accosted by the devil who offered to help him on the condition that he could claim the life of the first to cross the bridge. The pact was made but when the work was finished it was a dog that was the first to cross. As it did so, it mysteriously disappeared. From then on, Hugh said 'this bridge has acquired a certain spooky significance.'

Hugh was a bit shocked when I insisted on going into a gift shop where I bought a, not very skilful, watercolour of the Ponte della Maddalena painted by a local nun.

We climbed from the river level up through chestnut woods and through the lower part of Bagni di Lucca until we came to a tiny Piazza at the top. We left the car and walked up a steep path where Byron spent some months with his 'last attachment' Teresa Guicciolli. From there we could see a house that Shelley had rented in order to be nearby – close to another house where Montaigne had, reputedly, lived many years before that. Driving down we stopped again to see the English church. It had been built by subscription in Victorian times and was disguised as an Indo-Scottish castle. There was still some sort of trust to help maintain it although there were gaping holes in the floor. John pointed to a crooked wall-hanging that still held old hymn numbers. Ancient and Modern. Continuing down the Via Evangeline Whipple, we passed a sprawling villa, half hidden by walls and a wrought-iron gate where Evangeline had written *A Quiet Corner of Tuscany*. 'Not a very good book' Hugh said, 'but her family came here from Denver, Colorado and were great benefactors to the town.'

Bagni di Lucca had been the Simla of its day. The English who suffered from the excessive heat in Florence or on the coast swarmed there for the shade of the chestnut trees. Hugh told us that there was even a slip coach from the Rome express that took passengers directly there. The same slip coach brought a grouse lift to the town. 'There would be crates of them at the railway station by August 14th at the latest.'

As we reached the Protestant Cemetery where we had planned to have our picnic, the sky clouded over. John and Hugh wanted to show us the tomb of Ouida (the novelist Louise Ramé who took her own childish mispronunciation of her first name as her *nom de plume*). Ouida died of pneumonia in the severe winter of 1909 at the age of sixty nine. She was buried at Bagni di Lucca after years of poverty and near-blindness – deserted by all but her dog. The English consul of the time is said to have been moved by her bleak end and to have paid for her tomb, faithfully copied from the Della Quercia effigy to Ilaria del Carretto in the Cathedral in Lucca. Dog included.

Hugh said 'her novels were quite ridiculous. Percy enjoyed making fun of them.' He imitated Percy quoting from *Under Two Flags*, 'They all rowed fast but none faster than Guy.' John laughed and added 'That odious queen of Florentine society, Janet Ross, is said to have horse-whipped Ouida in the streets of Florence for libelling her in the novel *Friendship.*'

By the time the picnic moment arrived, the Tuscan heavens opened. We pulled our coats over our heads. Hugh covered the picnic basket as best he could and we belted up to a deserted chapel which, to our joy, turned out to be used for storing bales of hay. These we quickly rearranged to provide a table and benches – using rugs as a table-cloth. In no time we were very snug – looking out at a drenched Ouida and overhanging mountains half hidden in mist and beating rain. Surrounded, as we were, by chestnut woods, Hugh had decided that it would be appropriate to start with chestnut soup – kept hot in a large thermos.

When we returned to the Villa Marchio, John said 'Great Scott. That was enjoyable but we're glad it's over.'

14

The boys always sat at tea-time in the summer in the loggia that Nicky had sketched. Hugh would carry out the tea-tray – an exotic blend in a silver tea-pot over irregular paving stones. Hugh bought a BMW and drove it at a high speed as John cried 'mercy' at every bend. Hugh had a discreetly dashing side – with his James Bond cigarettes and love of good restaurants.

They introduced me to their friends – many in Florence; took me to lunch with Harold Acton at La Pietra – his startling renaissance villa outside Florence. Harold had known my parents in Shanghai before the war and greeted me with theatrical, high-toned, enthusiasm. 'Your dear mother bubbled over but, oh dear, your father was rather glum. John and Hugh tell me that you, like your mother, bubble over.' As we drove away, down the long,

87

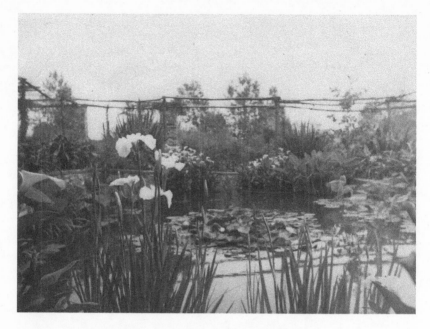

View on the lotus pond from Villa Marchio

cypress-lined, avenue, Hugh said 'That went very well. Harold enjoyed the Shanghai connection.' John said 'for moment I almost believed that he was going to tell you how much he had admired the slippery little ivory bodies of the oriental boys out there.' Hugh added 'Yes, the slippery little ivory bodies got him into trouble with the foreign service at the time.'

I also met John Pope-Hennessy (known as the Pope) and his companion Michael Mallon – then living in an apartment opposite the Pitti Palace. John Pope Hennessy, retired Director of the British Museum, struck me as cold and bloodless. He had poor manners and showed noticeable disdain when being introduced to me – until something struck him. The person he had loved best was his redoubtable mother – Dame Una. I can't imagine how – but he suddenly realised that she had been a great friend of my grandmother, Muriel Paget. Muriel, was an eccentric philanthropist and humanitarian and a biography of her had been written by Wilfred Blunt. That struck a chord and we became friends – not that I ever felt easy with him. Some time later John and Hugh were ostracised for nearly a decade by 'The Pope.' They had observed, in print, that when pursuing old altar pieces in Tuscan hill towns, he did not neglect 'the local flora and fauna – especially the fauna.' Personally I did not see that as particularly offensive but JPH didn't like it.

We dined with John and Thekla Clark in an ancient castle at Bagni a Ripoli. Thekla was a warm hearted American beauty – much loved by all and muse to W. H. Auden. Although always at ease with John and Thekla John said he felt 'cosier' when I went along with them to others. Maybe I had become homely.

Once they planned a whole day in Florence. Paintings, churches, lunch at La Pietra – more paintings and churches and supper at I Tatti with the director, Walter Kaiser. As we set out I overheard John saying to Hugh, 'Well. How will we manage? I mean Zanna is sure to spill food all over herself at lunch and, mercy, what will she look like with no opportunity to change clothes before supper?' John insisted that I tuck one of Harold's vast, white napkins under my chin as I ate. He, although on the scruffy side himself, always wanted me to be seen at my best. They boys had rather 'gone off' Harold by then. 'Too many photographs of royalty. He's become obsessed with them. It will lead to a very lonely old age.'

They kept their social life fairly quiet for fear of interfering with work but always encouraged old friends to stay with them at the villa. Francis and Larissa Haskell were among their favourite guests

– also Michael Napier (later Father Charles at the Brompton Oratory).

There was a handful of English neighbours (scoffingly known by outsiders as the Lucchese Inglese). I was soon introduced to them.

Very near Lucca lived Professor Michael Grant and his Swedish wife, Anne-Sophie. Michael was an English classicist and numismatist. He was also a well known populariser of ancient history. Books tumbled out of him. His wife was pretty and spoke in a sing-song voice. Her great claim to fame was that 'Greta Garbo once popped a strawberry into my mouth.'

Hugh pronounced that she wore 'VERY expensive scent.' For a while John and Hugh were friends of the Grants. After each Thursday morning, when the boys shopped in Lucca, they would go to their house to leave them the previous weeks' supply of the London *Times*. To start with they used to call in for a cup of coffee. Later they called in but didn't stop for coffee. As time went by they simply landed the newspapers on the Grants doorstep without even ringing the bell. Eventually they ceased going there at all. This caused great pain to Anne-Sophie who often telephoned me in England to say, 'What has happened? Have we offended the boys?' When I mentioned this to John he said 'Well. Mercy. We just didn't have the time for social day-time calls.' They were capable of a certain ruthlessness.

Also near Lucca lived Vernon Bartlett. He was, by then, a podgy elderly man and a well known author. By the time John and Hugh introduced me to him he was very lonely. His beloved wife, Nelly, had died and he used to walk through the streets of Lucca in the hope of bumping into someone he knew. Soon after I met him he had collected a second wife. He had met her on a cruise and didn't know her very well. Nor can he have cared for her much as he said to Hugh 'that woman uses more lavatory paper than anyone in the land but she has enormous tits.' After that we called her 'Tits' – but only in private.

Another neighbour was Lionel Fielden. He had caused a stir by writing a book called *The Natural Bent* – about his own homosexuality. He was on very familiar terms with his man-servant who caused trouble. The man-servant (whose name I have forgotten) sneaked into the Villa Marchio and told Gilda and Andrea what they ought to be paid. So – Lionel Fielden was then very much 'out.'

In a large house in the hills above the Villa Marchio, at Segromigno in Monte, lived a sad and lonely man. His name was Ronnie Emmanuel. He was Australian and Jewish; extraordinarily rich and a good amateur pianist. Not long before we knew him a law had been passed in Australia. It was called the Emmanuel Law and was drafted in order to prevent anyone, in the future, from owning as much land as this family did. Thousands of miles. Ronnie was tall, ill-favoured, kind and hospitable. He had a blood-curdling smile. John and Hugh always referred to him as 'the crocodile.'

He yearned for a companion in life but failed to find one. After many years at Segromigno in Monte, he threw himself out of an upper window and died. Poor Ronnie. John and Hugh were asked to go to the morgue to identify him. Not a pleasant experience.

One of the indigenous but honorary members of the 'Lucchese Inglesi' was Count Giovanni Tadini Buoninsegni Tobler. His mother had been a Tobler (of the Swiss chocolate family) and her fortune had been a great help to the Tadinis. John and Hugh were fond of him but always referred to him as 'Count Fosco' (from *The Woman in White*) – one of their favourite characters in literature. They half expected him to have tiny white mice crawling up his plump arms. John and Hugh took us to his weird house near Pisa. It had a very high and impressive facade with a double staircase leading up to the front door. Inside, however, it was extremely odd. Much of the major plan had never been completed. At the start it looked massive but, as you walked down the main passage to rooms that Giovanni lived in at the back, there was nothing at the sides or on top. The front hall was remarkable. As we went into it with John and Hugh, who had warned us in advance, we saw a round table that was covered with crowns and coronets, bejewelled and of many different sizes. It gave the distinct impression, pleasing to Giovanni, that many Kings and Queens, having left their crowns in the hall, awaited us. John and Hugh had told us that Giovanni spoke near-perfect and formal English – taught to him by a governess from Brighton. They hoped he would perform for us – and he did. There were several plums. He told us of having caught a train 'by the skin of its teeth' – of a neighbour as 'rather little fry' and he often said 'hats off to them' when delivering praise. Several 'mercys' came from John when we were shown bullet holes in the private chapel. They had been left by the Nazis after a battle which, towards the end of the war, raged through the village.

Our house, La Cavina, was some fifteen kilometres from Tofori. We would have liked to be a bit nearer to the Villa Marchio than that – but by then that side of the valley commanded high prices. When our repairs had been seen to, we sent a furniture van out from London and managed to squeeze in two Charles Howard arm chairs that John and Hugh had bought in London. Later I would take them cigarettes, Charbonnel et Walker chocolates, double-edged razor blades, marmite and gossip. Once I took them a Russell Hobbs electric kettle. They kept that in the sitting room and were then able to make their nightly cup of camomile tea without going down to the kitchen.

David Carritt arranged for a pug puppy to be sent out to them. They named it Tory and became besotted with him – as they did with a stray cat called Timmy. John, in particular, doted on Timmy but was somewhat disillusioned when 'he' had seven kittens in a suit-case in the attic. I'm not sure what became of the kittens but Timmy was almost forgiven for being a female cat. Definitely no further need for me to be a puppy or a kitten – but by then I was middle aged.

Hugh put a row of small glass jars on his desk, under a portrait of Canova – just behind his Olivetti typewriter and beside a permanently overflowing ash-tray. Most days he would pick a specimen of everything flowering in the garden and place each sprig in its own jar.

One summer I was at La Cavina when John rang unexpectedly early. He was usually a late riser but wanted to get to the telephone before their guest monopolised it. He said that they were getting to the end of 'our tether' with Derek Hill in the house. Derek had come, ostensibly, to paint their portrait. He did the job (very small on the lid of a cigar box and not a good likeness) in one afternoon but planned to stay at the villa for a good deal longer. John added, 'a bag of Mars Bars melted in his suit-case and he expected Lucia

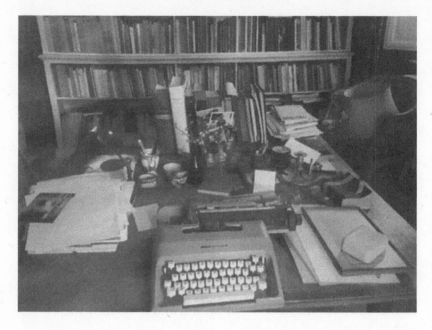

Hugh's desk

to sort it out for him.' Lucia was a stout and cheerful person who replaced the retired Gilda as cleaner in the house. John and Hugh wanted me to go there for lunch to help fill up the time as Derek was getting on 'our nerves.' When I arrived John took me, alone, into the garden. Hugh was working and Derek, as was his wont, stood firmly in John's study – tethered to the only telephone in the house. John had been frantic to talk to their publisher. 'Well.'

Lunch was quite jolly with Derek, who could be a very good companion when things went his way, in a happy mood – having fixed up the next leg of his Italian tour.

Hugh, though, was less jolly. He was always very careful about house-keeping and had discovered that Derek had raided the refrigerator in the night and had eaten all the cheese, butter and a

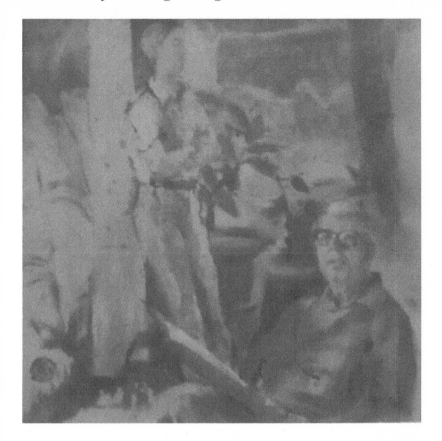

John and Hugh by Derek Hill

chocolate mousse – prepared in advance and intended for supper that evening. Later John said 'of course, in spite of his intolerable behaviour, we really are rather fond of the old thing.'

John and Hugh didn't much like the portrait on the cigar box but promised to leave it to me in their will. Now, with continued amusement, I look a the picture as it hangs in the hall of our Oxfordshire cottage.

95

15

By the late 1970s our four daughters had reached their teens and our Italian house became packed with their friends. I had never imagined that John and Hugh would enjoy noisy evenings on our terrace – but they often came over. Usually we had spaghetti and peaches from trays bought daily at the roadside. They were both amused by the excitement. Teenagers 'skinny dipping' in the very small swimming pool after supper – fire flies galore.

As time went by more boys began to arrive and, although John ogled a bit, Hugh remained calm and dignified. For those summer evenings, Hugh would wear a patterned shirt, no tie, cotton trousers and a pale linen jacket. John was always in his chef's trousers and crumpled shirt. From time to time I would renew the chef's trousers – buying them for him from a restaurant outfitters in Soho.

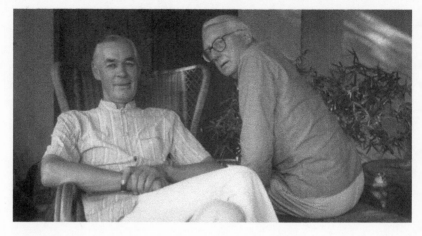

Hugh and John

Our great family friend, Rudolf Loewenstein – now Father Rudolf – has reminded me of one of those evenings at La Cavina.

'When I was a teenager I stayed there several times and greatly enjoyed it. It was the custom that, after the young ones had supper, we would go down to the village for an ice-cream and a chat with other children there. We always had to be back by ten o'clock and would then announce ourselves to the adults who were having a more leisurely dinner. Part of the announcing would result in our singing to them. Now My Mother-in-Law Is Dead – and a Beatle song or two – but, when we sang 'Oh! Dear! What Can the Matter Be? Three Old Ladies Got Stuck in the Lavatory' with added made-up verses we thought we were very daring.'

On one such evening John and Hugh dined with us. On returning from the village, the teenagers (including Rudolf) raced to my cupboard and returned to the table – wearing my frocks, high heeled shoes and summer hats – before bursting into song.

John and Hugh had never seen the like. John shook with

laughter and Hugh gently wiped his eyes.

One year our daughter, Lily, arrived at La Cavina with an enter-taining 'queer' friend from Oxford. He had a tremendous 'way' with older men who nearly always became besotted with him on sight. While he was staying with us he met John and Hugh and, ingeniously, found some method of slipping away on his own to visit them at the Villa Marchio. John admitted that they were really taken with him although – Hugh added – 'we didn't pounce.'

Pounce or not, they doted on the boy and arranged for the whole of the month of August, the following summer, to be spent in China with the new object of their affections. I was terribly put out. An entire summer holiday with John and Hugh away. They were our mainstay there and it seemed unthinkable that we were to do without them. When they returned we overlapped by a day or two and I visited them – allowing them to know that I had been displeased. Hugh handed me a large parcel – out of which emerged a magnificent, ancient Chinese silk skirt. It glimmered with blue and gold thread and fell in panels and pleats. They had bought it in Shanghai as a peace offering and it was accompanied by the words, spoken in unison 'we promise that it will never happen again.'

I often tried to picture them as they chose this skirt for me; fingering silks as they decided how to make amends. I have given the ancient skirt to my daughter, Lily, who had originally set the thing in motion by introducing the young charmer.

In spite of the fact that 'we didn't pounce', the episode caused John, in particular, much anguish and disturbance. Hugh remained steady but it had unnerved them both. Later they became straight-forward friends with the young man and things settled.

One day in the late 1970s John rang me and said 'Well. Who is

Lady Riddell?' I didn't know Sarah then but had known her husband and had known, too, that John Riddell was a baronet – so was able to give her an identity. She worked for a publisher and packager called John Calmann and John and Hugh were embarking on their great World History of Art. How old fashioned it now seems – to have introduced Sarah in that way. The boys had found it putting off. Sarah stayed with them several times during that period of editing and they became firm friends. Later, luckily for us, we too got to know and love her.

She remembers it well. 'The book was definitely John Calmann's idea. He went to Lucca to seal the deal and was terribly pleased when they agreed to do it. Soon after that he asked me if I would edit it. I was thrilled to pieces, of course, but tremendously daunted. Gosh – was I nervous when I was dropped at the villa for the first time. The thing I most remember was them asking me whether I knew "Zanna". I realised that this was the vital test I had to pass and, though I hadn't met her at the time, I bluffed because John (Riddell) had told me how much he liked her. They always seemed terribly excited when talking about "Zanna".'

'Much, too, was made of the "Lady" Riddell bit. They wanted to know what that was about and I think they were rather tickled. The first night I had to pull a rug onto the bed for warmth and the bedside light was so dim I couldn't read by it. In the morning John set me down in a room to the left of the house – while Hugh was mysteriously ensconced in his study, only emerging to cook lunch and dinner. Both were incredibly kind to me and I soon got the hang of it. John was the one I worked with (nine to one – then three to six). He was extremely organised about the book (notes, text; pictures all beautifully prepared.) He always made me laugh a

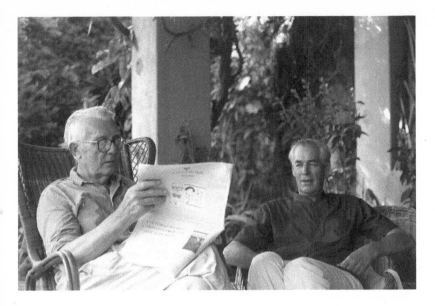

In the loggia

lot with his mischief. He was very easy with me but loved his vendettas with others. I was rather more circumspect with Hugh who didn't have John's easy way. It was all extraordinary and quite out of my experience. It was Hugh who produced the lion's share of the text. He was the more scholarly of the two and had an extraordinary range of knowledge of global art history. John wrote some chapters of the book, particularly about architecture for example, and did the remarkable job of organising and pulling the whole thing together. There was little I could add as an editor but if I did ever venture a comment it was always listened to and received appreciatively. They were model authors to work with.'

John Calmann was a larger-than-life and brilliant character; very showy and talkative – often embarrassingly so. In 1980 he went, for the second time, to stay for two nights at the Villa Marchio. John

101

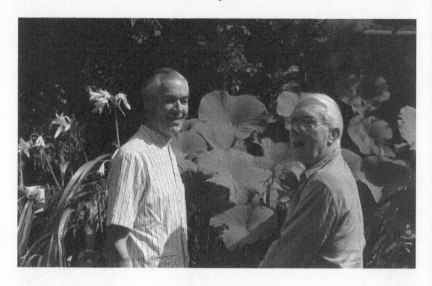

In front of the lily pond

and Hugh worked with their guest all day but feared he might expect some social life in the evenings. Italy was still playing it rather low-key after the previous decade of kidnappings. Showy cars, jewellery and fur coats were discouraged. John Calmann wasn't in a fur coat (it was very hot) but arrived in a vast blue Bentley *coupé*. John and Hugh were taken aback and asked me to go over. We were at La Cavina by then. I will never forget the flamboyant figure that greeted me as I mounted the steps. He began at once. 'I've just been staying with Maureen Dufferin in Sardinia. She calls her house Villa Costalotta.'

John and Hugh admired him professionally but were startled by his ceaseless flow of name dropping.

Hugh said 'I've been busy sweeping up the names he dropped on the terrace all afternoon.'

Fearful of his being bored, they asked if they could bring him to supper with me the following evening. I could deny them nothing and, of course, said yes. In fact I funked it – my table already being crowded with daughters and their friends. Instead we met at la Beita – barely more than a shed in a wood and run by friends of ours from the village. John Calmann was particularly lively that night and behaved outrageously – ordering the only waitress about in a high handed manner.

She was a middle-aged lady called Lina who had just been released from prison for breaking a plate on her husband's head – thus killing him. As though in a smart hotel, he flashed credit cards, unheard of in that remote spot, and was generally rather obstreperous. John and Hugh were quiet but mortified.

The next day John Calmann left the Villa Marchio and drove to the South of France to join his parents who had rented a house there for the summer.

I don't know the full story (perhaps no one does) of the horrible happenings of that day but it is believed that he gave a lift to a hitch-hiker who stabbed him to death. It seemed only moments since we had seen him at his noisiest and it sent out waves of shock and horror. Hideous for his family, of course, but also a fearful calamity for John and Hugh who had been much engaged in their professional association.

My dear friends, to their astonishment and horror, continued to be lionised. They had by now, published many great works and rich, culture craving, elderly ladies wanted to visit them. John and Hugh, like Harold Acton, Bernard Berenson (who John said was, 'like a little grasshopper') and Percy Lubbock in the old days, had become one of the prescribed Anglo-Tuscan sights. When they occasionally gave in – these ladies (Evangeline Bruce, Pamela Hartwell, Marietta

Tree amongst others) would turn up in chauffeur driven cars (chauffeurs petrified by the rough roads) hoping for high-class conversation. Hugh asked, over and over again, 'but WHY? Why on earth do they want to meet us? Can't they just read our books?' Later he enjoyed imitating them and their much rehearsed compliments. 'Oh! The lotus pond – the croaking of the frogs – the books – sheer heaven.'

Once when they were in London staying with Patrick Kinross, Hugh had to go alone to America. He was working on *The New Golden Land* (1975); based on how Europeans reacted to America from its first discovery up to the 1970s. It had been seen in many different ways – as an experiment, refuge, new Heaven or real Hell. It was almost unimaginable that John and Hugh were to be separated. Hugh had made it as clear as he could that he would rather John and I didn't meet when he was away. He did not think it wise that the balance of our triple friendship be disturbed. It had always been the same on Thursday mornings in Lucca. Hugh used to insist that I go with him to the fish-market and the bank – rather than leave me gossiping with John in the Art Deco bar in the Via Fillungo (the long thread). Nonetheless, on the morning after Hugh's departure for the USA, John rang me, small voiced, and said 'I'm a bit windy,' He was dead scared to find himself, probably for the first time in many years, to be unchaperoned.

Rather guiltily, we found ourselves defying Hugh's wishes and met for lunch at Simpsons. John still loved a good 'tuck in.' I adored the occasion but began to understand Hugh's veto. John liked intimacy and complained to me that Hugh would never allow him to help with cooking or washing up. 'Well. Sometimes I feel like throwing a saucepan at him.' That was the least of his indiscretions.

We had, also during Hugh's absence, arranged to take our teenage daughters to a performance of The Rocky Horror Show. We broke Hugh's law once again and asked John to come with us. It was a *risqué* show and a vast hit. All the rage. A musical with loud and catchy tunes telling the story of a naive and newly-engaged couple getting caught in a storm and finding themselves in the house of a mad, transvestite scientist who was in the act of unveiling his new creation – a sort of Frankenstein's monster in the shape of an artificially made, fully grown, muscular man called Rocky Horror – complete with blonde hair and a golden tan. The usherettes and ice-cream sellers were louche replicas of Rocky Horror and sidled up to members of the audience in the interval and as we left – caressing their faces. John enjoyed it to a point of near dementia – laughed until he sobbed and also wondered how, as he was certain to have to do, to break the news to Hugh of our double dealing.

When Hugh returned we all met for supper. He spoke firmly but not crossly. 'I've heard.'

That was all that was said of our treachery. It was never mentioned again.

16

In 1982 their book, *A World History of Art* – won the distinguished Mitchell prize. We went to the celebration in London where John and Hugh stood on the platform, speechless and bemused, like shy schoolboys, as their praises were sung. Hugh often said that he could hardly bear to see his own name on the back of a book – such was his modesty.

The same year, I, jointly with my cousin, Anne Tennant, brought out a book called *The Picnic Papers*. We collected picnic recipes together and bullied people to share their outdoor eating experiences. Despite Hugh's dislike of publicity, he turned in a marvellous piece for me.

Although they wrote to me often – they nearly always used the fax. It had been installed at the villa but fax paper was thin in those days so most of our correspondence has faded away. Mercifully the picnic book was published so I have Hugh's lyrical contribution in full.

He called it a 'White Picnic'.

'My ideal of a perfect picnic belongs to the 1950s, not later or earlier. Childhood treats were all very well in a Betjemanesque way. I too used to picnic where "the thrift grew deep and tufted to the edge." But today driving along the *Autoroute* south of Lyon, I read the sign *"Pique-nique jeux d'enfants"* as a warning rather than an invitation – though the phrase does have a ring of Verlaine about it. Most of my picnics nowadays are eaten on journeys across Europe by road. The company, limited to a maximum of four, is always that of old friends. The food, bought in the town where we spent the previous night, is also well tried – in Italy cold roast sucking pig and the best baked bread to be found anywhere in Europe now (much better than in France where it used to be so delicious), in Spain strongly flavoured ham, in Germany liver sausage, in France a selection of *pâtés, galantines* and *oeufs en gelée*. These picnics, however, are no more than brief affairs, intervals in a long drive, and never quite match to my or any other ideal. The *oeufs en gelée* too often prove to be hard-boiled, not *mollets*. The place where we stop attracts others almost immediately, and seldom seems in retrospect as congenial as the one we passed only a few minutes earlier or the one we noticed soon afterwards.

For me the perfect picnic must be incidental, just part of a journey through country beautiful in itself and, if possible, with literary or historical associations as well. My ideal picnic began to form twenty five years or so ago when I lived in Percy Lubbock's villa, Gli Scafari, near Lerici – a house of cool marmorial beauty perched on a rocky promontory above the crystalline blue of the still unpolluted Mediterranean, with a wide view of distant islands and the little fishing village of Porto Venere on the northern arm of the Gulf of La Spezia. The air was drowsy with literary associations. Percy himself had been at Cambridge with E. M. Foster – "poor old Morgan" as he often remarked, "he never quite knew the right people." Later he had been a disciple of Henry James, whose voice and conversation he could mimic when well-primed after dinner, and, for a time, one of Edith Wharton's "young men" – though he was banished from her little court when he married another wealthy cosmopolitan blue-stocking. Only a few hundred yards away D. H. Lawrence had spent the winter of 1913-14 in a four-roomed pink cottage on the shore of "a little tiny bay shut in by rocks, and smothered by olive woods that slope down swiftly." Beneath Gli Scafari there was a huge arching grotto, one of those, we liked to think, that Shelley had explored by boat during the last weeks of his life when he lived at San Terenzo on the other side of Lerici. Byron, on his way from Pisa to Genoa in October 1823, stopped at Lerici for a few nights and made himself ill by swimming far out to sea with Trelawny and eating a large dinner while treading water – one of the most bizarre picnics on record. Next year he was to sail along the same coast on his last voyage to Missolonghi. But, as we watched from the loggia at the passage of shipping out at sea or making for harbour at La Spezia or Porto Venere there was another figure from the past who haunted our imagination – Walter Pater.

I had first read *Marius the Epicurean* at school and thought it, as did the young Max Beerbohm, a marvellous "tale of adventure, quite as fascinating as *Mr Midshipman Easy*, and far less hard to

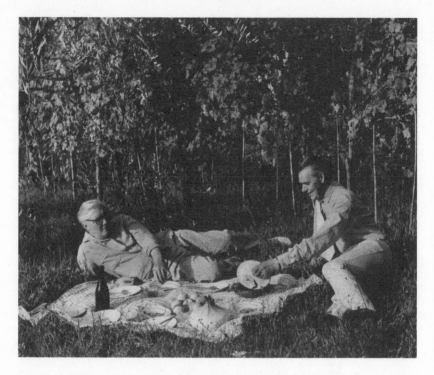

John and Hugh at a picnic, 1983

understand because there were no nautical terms in it." At Lerici I found myself near Marius's country. His villa, White Nights, was among the hills a few miles inland. Pater wrote that 'the traveller, descending from the slopes of Luna even as he got his first view of the Port-of-Venus would pause by the way, to read the face, as it were, of so beautiful a dwelling place, lying away from the white road, at the point where it began to descend somewhat steeply to the marsh-land below.' Each of the windows of Marius's tower chamber framed a landscape, 'the pallid crags of Carrara, like wildly twisted snow-drifts above the purple heath; the distant harbour with its freight of white marble going to the sea; the lighthouse

110

temple of 'Venus Speciosa' on its dark broadland and the long-drawn curves of white breakers,' The description is circumstantial enough to suggest that Pater, who could have passed this way when he went to Pisa, had a particular spot in mind. To find it became the object of many excursions and picnics.

Near the little village of Fosdinova there are several places which almost match Pater's description. From there one can see the Carrara Mountains, uncannily like those in the background of the Mona Lisa which inspired one of Pater's over-familiar purple passages. Glimpses may be caught of an ancient amphitheatre among vine-yards, all that remains above ground of the city of Luni from which Carrara marble was exported throughout the Roman Empire. But to find a point from which Porto Venere can also be seen is difficult. We never succeeded in locating it. If found, this would be the place for a perfect, truly Epicurean picnic.

Special food would, of course, be eaten; food of a preciosity to suit the occasion and predominantly white. We should begin with fish, cod, fillets of sole or shelled scampi and a very pale mayonnaise. Then there might be chicken breasts or quails, stuffed with white truffles and wrapped in the most delicately streaked bacon, lightly fried, accompanied by a white salad such as sometimes served in Italy in early spring – raw fennel cut into little strips, celery, chicory and paper-thin flakes of turnip sprinkled over with violet flowers to delight both eye and palate. To end we should have a cheese mousse of the type the cook at Gli Scafari used to prepare, firm yet crumbly to the fork and wonderfully light, composed mainly of ricotta (ewe's milk cheese) but according to a recipe I have never been able to trace. We should drink a dry white wine, Verdiccio, from the Marche. And afterwards, until the sun

111

sinks into the sea, we would read Pater's "oft-read tale" again, from the edition printed on hand made paper with title page designed by Herbert Horne, the biographer of Botticelli and one of the last Anglo-Italians of whom Pater might have wholly approved. But the place has not been, and may never be, found. So my perfect picnic remains an untarnished ideal – forever cold and still to be enjoyed.'

The piece was accompanied by a photograph of John and Hugh eating on their tufty lawn at the Villa Marchio. It is framed and hangs on my wall today. It was astonishingly kind of Hugh to take so much trouble on my behalf but he refused to be thanked. 'I much enjoyed writing about food for a change.'

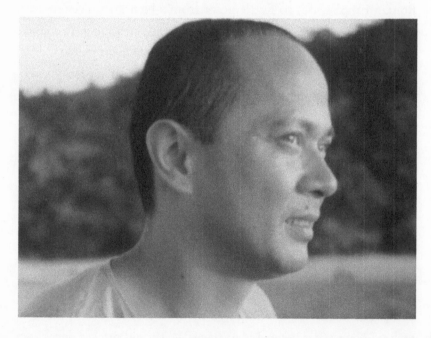

Carl Kraag

John said 'We really think that a picnic should be for two people only.'

That year things changed for the even better. John and Hugh were clearly excited about something and raced over to tell us – the day we arrived in Italy. They had, in Lucca, met two young men, Valter Fabiani (born and bred in Lucca) and Carl Kraag – half Dutch and half Thai. They had learnt that the two ran an antique shop in the medieval street, Via Battistero, near the cathedral of San Martino. On one of the boys' Thursday shopping days (after having been introduced to Carl and Valter at an oriental exhibition in the town) they had walked along the cobbled street and peeped in through the window where they saw the handsome Valter sitting

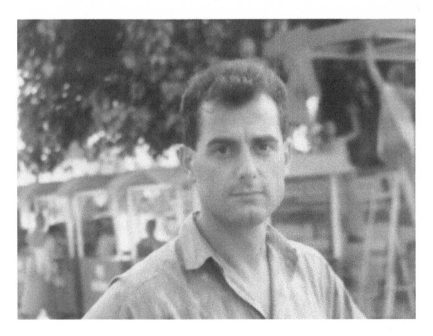

Valter Fabiani

113

and reading *The Portrait of a Lady* – in English. 'Well', John said, 'imagine an English antique dealer reading Dante in Italian.' Hugh said 'they are both perfectly charming.'

They were determined to introduce us and took us to the shop. It was filled with delights and we much enjoyed the meeting. When we left John turned to Nicky and said 'Aren't they dishy?' Nicky answered 'I don't really know about "dishy" but I did think they were very nice.'

John and Hugh had become increasingly fond of our daughters and had arranged for the eldest, Clara, to work for their great friends, John and Thekla Clark in their art-history photographic business in Florence. She spent many weekends at our house, La Cavina, and formed a close friendship with Carl and Valter – as did we and as, most certainly, did John and Hugh. The new friendship made a vast difference to their lives there. On Thursdays they were able to leave parcels in the shop, learn about goings on in Lucca – concerts and exhibitions – and to visit the pair in their Palazzo apartment in Piazza San Salvatore that looked out over a Roman bath, a dark enticing church and an ancient wine store.

Happy as those times were, nothing could prevent disaster from striking. John and Hugh returned from a trip to Bologna one evening to find that their house had been catastrophically burgled. Bad enough for anyone but, for them with their quiet, ordered, trusting lives, it was a calamity. The robbers had filled two lorry loads; a valuable Scagliola table, busts, lamps, drawings, china, the two rare shell-shaped grotto chairs and many of Hugh's mother's possessions.

The dining room walls had been decorated with blue and white china plates and dishes. They had all gone. John and Hugh were deeply haunted by it and became suspicious of strange faces in the neighbourhood. It was after that that the house began to slide. They were fearful of outsiders and put off getting repairs seen to. Tiles chipped and loosened, wiring became treacherous and, notwithstanding the cosiness of the great log fire in winter and the excellent food – the house began to look dilapidated. The ground floor flooded twice but they didn't get the damage seen to and fungus spread over the lower walls. The basement lavatory seized up and remained stinking and silted until this day.

No two people could ever have found a robbery harder to recover from. Fortunately some of the better pieces had been photographed and, by a series of odd coincidences, the Scagliola table was spotted in an antique shop in Florence and, after many trials,

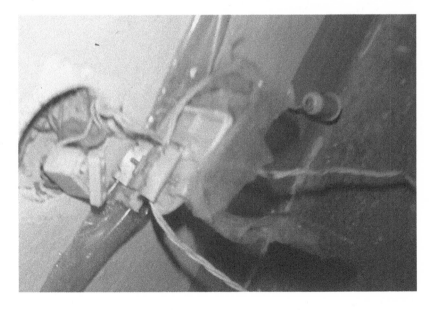

Wiring at Villa Marchio

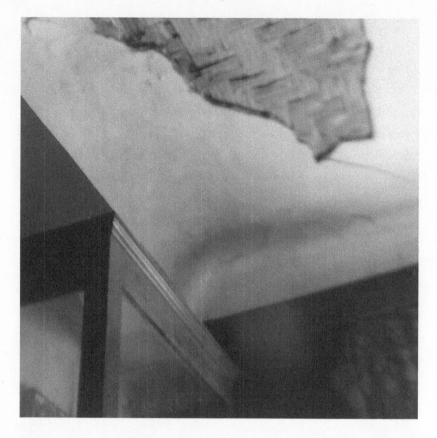

Ceiling in the study

recovered. John and Hugh had to appear at the hearing of the crooked antique dealer and found the experience harrowing.

I scoured English junk shops and drove to Italy with dozens of blue and white plates to restore the look of the dining room. Of course they were of poorer quality than the originals but the colour was right.

Things settled but they remained fearful for many years and John never fully recovered his peace of mind.

17

John and Hugh did continue to go to London but were now always anxious about leaving the house unguarded. Luigi, their scrawny neighbour, did his best – strolling around with a giant torch, but they decided that they needed someone to live in when they were away. They found a fellow – nice enough – but Hugh hated leaving anyone there as much as he hated leaving the place empty. The house-sitter always had to overlap with them when they left or returned and Hugh, in particular, couldn't bear that. 'It's not like getting home – finding him there and having to talk to him', John complained. 'He isn't even dishy.' Nonetheless the 'non-dishy' house-sitter came in very useful as John and Hugh, besides going to London, travelled widely during the winters – particularly in the East. I have stacks of post cards they sent me. I think John must

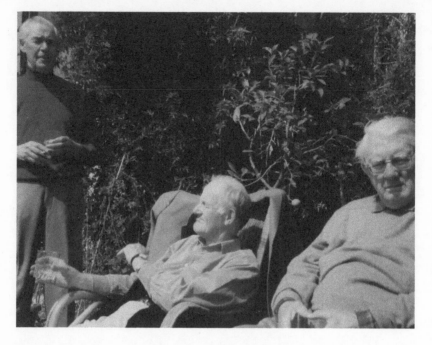

Hugh, Nicky, and John, 1990s

have, occasionally, given Hugh the slip – since some are from him alone. Those ones were nearly always of beautiful boys bathing on beaches – often in Thailand.

In the 1980s during a London spell, we were, all of us, invited to dinner by Jayne Wrightsman – the widow of an immensely rich oil magnate. She knew an extraordinary amount about eighteenth-century French pictures, furniture and china and owned a great deal of it. We had all met her with John Pope-Hennessy in Florence and she, it transpired, had much admired the rare books library designed by Nicky for the philanthropist, Paul Getty. She wanted to lure John and Hugh to her glamorous apartment that overlooked Green Park and we were used as bait to catch them.

The four of us went up in the lift. A maid in a frilly apron showed us in as Jayne Wrightsman cooed 'here comes the gang.' I don't think Hugh liked that much – the idea of being part of a gang. The place was filled with masterpieces – Renoirs and Cézannes – I felt I'd seen most of them on post-cards.

The hostess sat between Nicky and John on a sofa and flattered Nicky about the Getty library. 'When my ship comes in I'm going to send for you.' John whispered to me, 'I rather thought that ship HAD come in.'

It was the sort of fairly formal occasion that Hugh disliked. They enjoyed the 'tuck in' though and marvelled at the pudding. Ice-cream in the shape of a water-melon. The colours were made with pistachio and strawberry – the pips were dots of chocolate. Later we learnt, by comparing notes here and there, that it turned out to be her signature pudding – served wherever she happened to be.

After supper we saw, through an open door, a maid in a cap and apron as she slipped upstairs with Jayne Wrightsman's hot-water-bottle. I expect she needed one as she was unnaturally thin. I guess it's a chestnut but once, when she was ill, the joke was that 'Jayne Wrightsman has eaten something.'

'A relief that's over', Hugh said as we went down in the lift.

I stayed with them regularly at the Villa Marchio. They tended to put their work behind them in the evenings – with unscholarly me at any rate – and enjoyed talking of other things. John was nearly always indignant about something; often a news topic he'd heard on the wireless or an altercation he'd had with a publisher. We did, though, naturally touch on what they were doing – looked at possible book covers, read reviews together and discussed future projects. Once I asked them why they showed so little interest in the work of Henry Moore. Hugh said 'We think he was greatly overrated and probably ruined as an artist by Kenneth Clark who we did NOT care for.'

In 1985, our lively daughter, Rosie, was rusticated for a term by her college. Something to do with substances. I promised the head of her college that we would keep her as distanced from drugs as we were capable of doing for the rest of the term.

I was in the bath when Rosie burst in to tell me that she intended to spend what time remained with her cousin in Amsterdam. I knew a bit about both the cousin and Amsterdam and refused her permission. Rosie was aghast. I had always been hopeless at refusing anyone anything. We both exploded.

That night I told John, on the telephone, about our distressing goings on. He barely paused before saying 'Why not send her out here? We love all your daughters and she would be perfectly safe with two old queers.'

Rosie was horrified by the plan but we set off, in my little green Fiat, for Tofori.

She, Rosie Johnston (now Rosie Smith) has written me her account of what happened there.

'John and Hugh were a feature of our family life since my earliest memories. As a child they seemed to me to be distant and refined – unapproachable in the shrieking, giggly ways of my three sisters and me as we trailed about Lucca nagging Mum for ice-creams or pastries from our favourite *pasticceria*. Visiting John and Hugh, which we often did, at the beautiful, crumbling Villa Marchio, was not an easy outing for us. They were erudite art historians – not much fun if you're obsessed by snogging and discos. They didn't seem wildly interested in us although they were obviously devoted to Mum and she to them. I remember *prosecco* on the loggia outside their house – Hugh smoking his thin, brown cigarettes and John, an altogether more cuddly proposition, smiling behind his round glasses. They were there, always there and there was a dim understanding that our frequent trips to our own small house were because of them. I never imagined that I would develop my own friendship with them, rather as my mother had done, in an entirely unexpected way.'

'I was trouble, lock, stock and loaded barrel. On this particular occasion I had been rusticated from university for taking drugs in term time. I had important exams coming up and Mum and Dad were at a loss. Keeping me at home would be hard work with windows begging to be climbed out of, friends willing to pick me up in the middle of the night to go clubbing. I wanted to go to Holland but that had been vetoed. The pressure to keep me on the straight and narrow was immense and Mum was at her wits end – as she told John during a telephone conversation.'

'"Send her here", John said. "She'll be out of harm's way. No car. She can revise for her exams with no distractions."'

'The solution was jumped on. I was informed that Mum would drive me to John and Hugh's, stay for a night or two then leave me there for three weeks on my own. This didn't fit with my ideas at all. I could stay with friends in London and revise there. Much more convenient surely? '

'Our drive to John and Hugh's took two days, with the usual stop at Bourg-en-Bresse. It was April – too cold to eat outside at the station hotel, so we had our steak *frittes* in the large nineteenth-century dining room. A warty man with glasses took

121

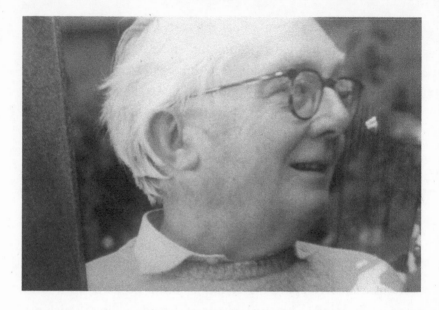

John, 1990s

an interest in us; wanting to know where we were from. We were half way down our *carafe* of house red and talking in O-level French. When we got to our room there was a letter that had been slipped under the door. It was a violently passionate declaration of love from warty to my mother. She had that effect, often on slightly strange people, who fell for her at sight. I wasn't crazy about the idea of Warty breathing all over me but I was mildly irritated at being bypassed by my mother. We got the giggles and went to bed.'

'When we arrived at the Villa Marchio, John and Hugh were there to greet us. It was dark, the evening damp and unlit by fireflies at that time of year. We ate in their dining room – the table only fit for six at the most. Hugh did the cooking and I seem to remember fish pie and pears stewed in red wine.'

'My bedroom, along a freezing corridor, had a loose electrical wire that crackled blue sparks if a switch, somewhere in the recesses of the house was turned on. The single bed and shuttered windows were perfect for scholastic asceticism, but I wanted my thick blanket and rose patterned wallpaper. I could hardly think of anything to say at dinner. Mum and "the boys" as they were often known, talked of literary friends and goings on in the Lucchesia. I couldn't think how we were going to manage without Mum. I was writing an essay on *Paradise Lost* and just starting to delve into John Wilmott, Earl of Rochester – but knew that my fumbling observations would be no match for these two seething lemons.'

'Mum stayed for two nights and was gone. I was nervous and awkward. What the hell were we to talk about? That first dinner without Mum, John got straight down to business. "Have you been to any gay clubs?" Two ways to go here, I thought. Deny any knowledge of Heaven, Maitresse, Tuesday Night at the Hippodrome. Or give 'em the whole enchilada? We sat up talking for hours. What kind of people went to such spots? Did I have gay friends? (indeed I did). What did they wear? What was the music like? (Donna Summer. It was the eighties). I was limbering up, really enjoying myself. The twenty black men in gold *lame* jock straps at the Hippodrome, the rubber and leather of Maitresse under the arches at King's Cross. What had I worn? Where did I buy it? I was in my element, describing the two piece rubber ensemble I'd bought at Kensington Market. The boys, who I thought only talked about art, antiques and architecture were replaced by wide-eyed, giggling vicarious clubbers. It was perfect. After dinner, they asked if I liked opera. Thanks to our early trips

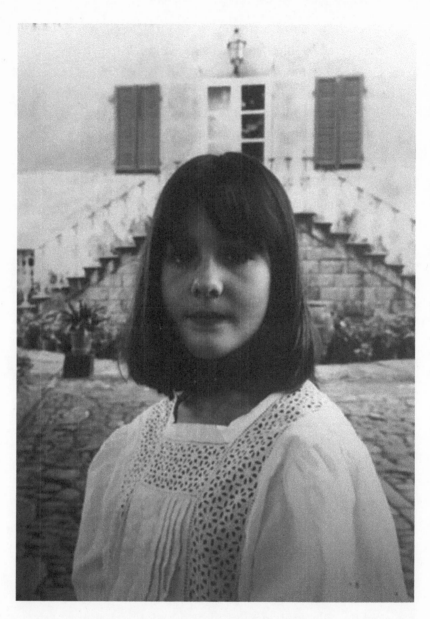

Rosie at the Villa Marchio, photo by Derry Moore, 1987

with Mum and Dad to Torre del Lago, Puccini was a favourite. Verdi followed on from that and Mozart, too, was a regular on my Sony Walkman. John and Hugh had other ideas. They had just bought a 'woofer' which they talked about with as much excitement as Gay Night at Frazzle. They made me sit with my back to the stereo, Hugh on my right and John opposite. The first notes of the Prelude to Tristan and Isolde and I was hooked and netted into a new world. John suggested highlights from Wagner to get me started; the Liebestod, Tristan and Isolde's act two love duet, then Lohengrin's great revelation aria. Over the next few weeks I was immersed in Wagner, Korngold, Puccini's Edgar, Gianni Schicci, Berg's Wozzek. Hugh told me, sternly, to leave the Ring until I was sixty 'or it will take over your whole life.' We listened to symphonies. Shostakovich's sensational second. Brahms's third (to get me started apparently). Piano concertos played by Brendel and Horowitz. It was, for me, the most astonishing introduction to a world of music that I've never left.'

'On the fourth or fifth day, John announced that friends were coming for dinner; two gentlemen antique dealers from Lucca. Oh well, I thought, it's been lovely having John and Hugh all to myself but inevitably some dry old fogies were bound to show up sooner or later.'

'Enter Carl Kraag and Valter Fabiani. I sat up. They were young, incredibly attractive, Carl as smooth as an egg with his Asian blood. Valter as good looking as an Italian man could be, with his spotless white t-shirt and, well, cool linen jacket. We fell on each other instantly knowing that we would be friends for the rest of our lives – which we have been. John and Hugh didn't bat an eyelid when Carl rolled a joint. I was beginning to wonder if this was quite what Mum had in mind when she took me to The Boys for sheltered seclusion – but forgot about that when Carl and Valter asked me to go to Frau Marlene's with them – a transvestite nightclub on the Lido di Camaiore strip. John and Hugh were obviously longing for me to go so they could quiz me about it the next day.'

'Frau Marlene's kicked my London clubbing experiences into the long grass. The tranny scene had exploded in Italy – beautiful he/shes in sequinned hot pants and platform shoes. One I remember in Dutch national costume with plaits and brightly rouged cheeks. Carl, Valter and I danced all night and they tipped me home at five in the morning. I didn't lie in for long. The Boys had breakfast in their rooms but I had promised to meet them at nine thirty and I knew that, John in particular, would be bursting with excitement. I regaled them with details that I could only hazily remember.'

It was many months before John and Hugh quite came clean to me about the details of Rosie's time there. It took Rosie even longer to spill the beans.

By the middle of the 1990s John's sight began to worsen. He was brave and took to listening to Talking Books. They were beautifully done on tape. John's favourites were *The Chronicles of Barsetshire*, sublimely read by Timothy West. He particularly liked the bits about Mrs Proudie. He often re-wound the tape to hear again the unrivalled moments when Mrs Proudie's skirt was caught in the castor of the sofa on which lay La Signora Madeline Vesey Neroni. 'Gathers were heard to go, stitches to crack, plaits to fly open, flounces were seen to fall, and breadths to expose themselves; a long ruin of rent lace disfigured the carpet and still clung to the vile wheel on which the sofa moved.' I much admired the way John enjoyed these new props. Many in his position would have sat back and moaned. He did no such thing. Sometimes John asked me to read to him. He had always had a feeling for German literature and the first book he picked out was *Effie Briest*. He was shocked that I had never read, or even heard of, it. A realist novel written by Theodore Fontane in 1896, it was one of John's favourite works of fiction; a mysterious, sad, slightly creepy and poetic book.

Another that I read to him was Goethe's *Elective Affinities*; also one of John's top choices. That had been written in 1809. It was based on the metaphor of human passions being regulated by the laws of chemistry. I found it gloomy, slightly incomprehensible but rather marvellous. John revelled in it and my mind went back to the early days of our getting together when we read aloud to Percy at Lerici.

Hugh cared and cooked for John with uncomplaining efficiency and, often by word of mouth from John, their work was able to continue. Hugh, though, was already doing a lot independently – mainly on his Canova research. In the evenings they listened to classical music on CDs. Their collection of these had become immense and esoteric.

They enjoyed visits, particularly from young people who demanded no reciprocal hospitality. They couldn't bear people 'who think they should invite us back.' In a summer month, my pretty niece, Amelia Gatacre, visited them. She remembers it well. 'I went with two friends (boys) on motorbikes. It was in the early nineties. My friends were loath to drive their precious bikes down the bumpy road so we walked, in the stupefying heat, clad in leather from head to toe. When we got there Hugh, beautifully dressed in white and with tea prepared by the lotus pond, asked us why we were on foot. My friends replied that they had been put off by the rocky road. Hugh said 'Ah but I drive my BMW up and down it at least twice a week with no trouble at all.' Sadly John's sight was very bad but they were both welcoming and wonderful company.'

One afternoon we discussed the making of the boys' wills. They had each, of course, made reciprocal ones but wondered what to do when the survivor died. They very much wanted that to be a joint decision.

Valter Fabiani, who we all by now loved and respected, was, between us, decided on to be their eventual and official '*erede.*' He was Italian and would know how to deal with authorities. He was years younger than all of us and knew about works of art – besides being loveable, trustworthy and more than capable of dealing with any 'wish lists.' It turned out to have been an excellent choice.

The boys had to stop travelling – even visiting London – but John went on enjoying telephonic chats and was able, with a struggle, to write letters – as he sat almost on top of his typewriter.

18

In 1997 I had a bad car crash. As I drove along a bumpy road, my car flew into the air and headed for the wrong side of the road. I had no control. I was sure to die. I shouted 'I'm sorry everybody' – very loud. When all was still – blood spurted from my hand, head and right arm. I was in the back of the upturned car. Trapped. I had not worn a seat-belt for the short journey. I was hunched up and my ribs hurt horribly. I heard them scrunch. I tried to hold my hand up but there was no space. Blood swirled everywhere and, although conscious, I began to weaken. A car stopped and a young man jumped out and ran towards me. One look and he said 'I'll go for help.'

'If you do' I said, 'I'll die. Help me stop the bleeding. Get my cardigan off. We must make a tourniquet.' I had done a first aid course the year before. Poor boy. It can't have been easy through the shattered upside-down window but, undoubtedly, my life was saved that way. Soon I was in an ambulance and in completely awful pain. I screamed and yelled and swore that I was dying and urged them to hurry. I remember the bell. I was in hospital and my hand was being looked at. Two men, both with beards, said words like 'serious injury' and 'get her down to the infirmary.' Somebody asked me if I minded that they cut me out of my dress – a pink, stripy one from India. Then they asked me what I wanted done with my bra and pants. The cardigan-cum-tourniquet wasn't mentioned although it was a lovely blue cashmere one. Then I was asked what they were to do with a surrealist ring I wore on my right hand. Was my right hand, then, a part of my past? The ring, a prosthetic surgical human eye replacement; a green eye staring from a silvery surround had, maybe, no longer any finger to adorn. Little did I realise, when I was given that ring, that the words 'prosthetic,' 'surgical.' and 'replacement' were to become a part of my new vocabulary. Hitherto I had only used them in heartless jest. I had to have two fingers on my right hand removed. Sixty stitches had been sewn across my forehead. An object was placed in my rib cage (pierced lungs) and heaven knows what else happened to me.

After sweltering some weeks in a pulsating ward, I was taken home but needed nursing. Nicky kept John and Hugh in close touch almost by the day. I have still got letters of sympathy that arrived but, here, only quote the ones that had relevance to John and Hugh.

Jim Lees Milne sent a copy of his latest book *Ancient as the Hills* (for once not rude about me) containing a characteristic and not wholly sincere inscription 'To darling Susanna with love from her faithful old hound Jim. 1997. Instructions; to be taken day or night in as large or small doses as the patient thinks fit; and keep out of reach of those in second childhood lest they wreak revenge on the author.'

The book was accompanied by an equally characteristic letter. 'I am re-reading the letters of those learned book-worms Hart-Davis and Lyttleton in which they agree that the purest prose ever written in the English tongue is in Percy Lubbock's *Earlham*. I know you knew him well. When I did read it I found it rather dry and lifeless. I must try again. What would John and Hugh pronounce?'

John and Hugh pronounced it 'a great work but soporific.'

John sent me a copy of Roy Strong's new book for my amusement – writing on the card that came with it – 'he must be half off his head.'

John also wrote a letter – not a fax. 'We are so glad you are over the worst now. It must have been ghastly. We have been thinking of you ALL THE TIME and hoping and praying it will go well eventually. We were so impressed when Nicky told us of the poor young man who saved your life at the roadside. Was he dishy? We'll telephone at five o'clock – your time – and hope to talk with you. If you're at the hospital that afternoon (Nicky told us that you have to go most days) of course we'll ring again. The other night, when we telephoned and left a message on your machine, we were going out to this *vernissage* of Carl and Valter. It was a HUGE success – you would have loved it – lots of people drinking champagne – so many that they spilled onto the street. The Via Battistero was packed with people chattering. I've got greatly taken by Barbara Vine – do you read her? I can't remember. She may be old news for you but we'd never heard of her until recently and she's *frightfully* good as the Pope would have said. *Dearest* Zanna. Lots of love and *bacci*. Of course come here to recuperate. Perhaps, if you need nursing, you'd be better at La Cavina with Roberta to look after you. We're not much good at nursing but would visit you every day.'

After just over a month I did fly to Pisa – arm in plaster and a sling – and very wobbly. John and Hugh were at the airport to meet me – anxiety scratched over their faces. John was dressed as a snow man with a red woolly scarf and hat. I had knitted them for him a year or two earlier. Their car bulged with fruit from their garden and with flowers and tomatoes. They drove me to our house where Roberta took charge with noisy tenderness and where the sun, soon to disappear in favour of remorseless rain, was shining. Carl and Valter brought a picnic supper that very first evening – roast chicken and an astounding pudding from a fanciful Lucca bakery. Roberta took full charge of me and my needs. John rang every morning to ask if she'd washed my hair yet. He was convinced she was in love with me and wanted to hear of every detail of her nursing skills. She drove me to the Villa Marchio where I dined and, bravely, spent the night. It was terrific. The evening sped along and Hugh cooked two of my favourite things. *Boeuf Bourguinon* and grilled peaches with melted brown sugar on top. When I got to bed, though, my head went round and round. So fast that I couldn't see. I was scared and bunged with drugs.

In the morning, after Lucia had brought me breakfast – something very unexpected happened. John came and sat on my bed. He said 'We have been thinking. Your hand. We have decided that you should make a feature of it. Perhaps a very colourful glove with beads dripping from it.' My hand was dreadfully mangled and ugly. I had wondered how to face life with such disfigurement. It

132

was excellent advice and to some extent I have taken it. Colourful gloves at any rate. I didn't ever get round to dripping beads.

One morning Rosie rang me very early. She was in the USA and world news reached her before it got to our neck of the woods. The Princess of Wales had been killed in a car crash with her lover in Paris – escaping the *paparazzi*. I couldn't but think that, if someone had to be killed in a car crash, I was glad it had been her and not me. I was advised not to say that in public – taking into account the uproar of sentimentality her death began to cause.

Nicky had arrived by then and that night we went to dinner with Carl and Valter. The food was designed so that I was to have no cutting up to do. John and Hugh were there and Hugh said 'All right. You can talk about it tonight but NEVER again.' They were doggedly unmoved by the death of the Princess.

A day or two later we met again – John, Hugh, Nicky and my maimed self – for lunch at the Villa Reale – a short distance from all of us. It was a splendid place. An ancient house but renovated and much enlarged by Elisa Baciocchi – sister of Napoleon – who bought it, as well as neighbouring land, in 1806. Grottoes, topiary theatre, cascades and ponds – swans, avenues and much colour. When the Pecci Blunt family took over the property in 1923 they added, among other comforts, an Olympic-sized swimming pool with bright blue tiles and a Chinese Chippendale diving board.

To meet us on the steps was our mutual friend, Camilla McGrath (one of the Pecci Blunt daughters). Camilla, a dear and comical person, was there with her more formal sister Letizia Buoncompagni. Before leading us into the house Camilla whispered, 'Please. Not a word about the Princess of Wales at lunch. My sister thought she was a saint and I think she was a

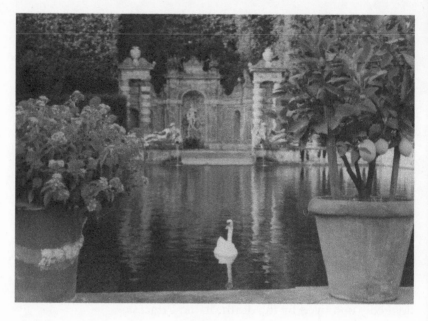

Villa Reale

whore.' John and Hugh found that order easy to obey. John still wore his woolly scarf and hat in my honour but Hugh had taken to light Indian suits with Nehru collars.

Not long after that I returned to England and innumerable operations.

By the end of the century John began to suffer from back ache. Sometimes the pain was intolerable. He was diagnosed as having bone cancer and hopes of his being with us for long began to dwindle – not, though, his courage or that of Hugh. By the spring of 2001 John became very ill. He was bed-bound and Hugh took him every meal – on a tray – up forty steps from the desperately battered kitchen. Hugh, by then, was seventy five and found it exhausting. By the end of May, Hugh, sounding apprehensive, rang

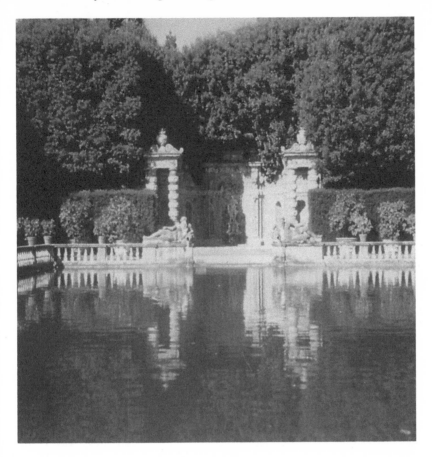

Villa Reale

me in England. 'I'm very much tempted to ask you to come out.' I said 'Why, for the first time in your life, don't you give way to temptation?' He did give way – so off I went.

Things were sad at the villa. John was uncomfortable in bed; barely able to speak. He looked different as he no longer wore specs. I remember Hugh saying 'John. Zanna's here.' I held his hand and he smiled with great sweetness. It was then that I realised

135

that, in some ways, women are better in the sick room than men. Hugh had never heard of a cup with a lip and sploshed water all over John's face every time he gave him something to drink. Nor did he know of invalid pillows and John floundered in his bed. Their beloved Doctor Nottoli came every day and told me, with great solemnity, that John had only a few days to live. Hugh was very calm, sad and hard-driven. Piera, from one of the cottages, came to jab pain killing injections into John's thin, white arms. Lucia (their more than loyal helper) sobbed and the garden was overgrown. 'My little jungle' Hugh now called it.

John died on an early June morning. Hugh must have been with him as he knocked on my bedroom door and said 'Zanna. It's all over.' Later in the day it was very hot. Things, including funerals, happen fast in Italy. Within hours a small temple had been erected in the lower hall and John lay in it – looking handsome and happy. He was smartly dressed and wearing his old Rugby tie. Piera, Lucia and other local ladies sat with him – and continued to do so throughout the two days and nights before his burial. They were surprised and a little shocked, we realised, that Hugh and I did not wish to do the same. We ate and even laughed in the next room. We were, after all, English.

During breakfast, that first day, as the temple was being put up, I warned Hugh that we must be on our guard. Newspapers and art magazines would soon be telephoning wanting help with obituaries. Hugh said, 'tell them NO. I don't want any. John would have hated it.' Hugh was astonishingly unworldly. As if obituaries could possibly be prevented. The calls began but Hugh was unco-operative. There were, naturally, many glowing testimonies – all over the place – England, Italy, USA. Hugh did, though, give the impression of being pleased when, later, he read them.

As for the funeral arrangements. I had no car there and Hugh, although outwardly calm, was shaky and certainly not capable of driving up the wiggly road to the church at Tofori where John was to be buried.

The news of John's death was spreading and it became clear that the funeral was likely to be attended by a great many people; academics from Florence and Pisa – and from far further afield. I asked Hugh what we were to do with them all when they came back to the villa after the service. He answered 'There are two cartons of fruit juice in the refrigerator. That should be enough.'

I rang the trusty Roberta who rushed over with a car-load of food and wine. She was (still is) bustling, noisy and efficient as she laid everything out under the giant cedar tree in stifling heat. She then drove me and Hugh very fast, in her rattling, red car up scary roads to the church.

All the church doors were open and mountains showed in the distance. The church was packed with very hot people. John was buried in the cemetery at Tofori – a delightful place in which to end up. Hugh is now there. Back everyone crowded, Muriel Spark among them, to the Villa Marchio. There was much respect in the air. Much sadness too.

Later, as we dined, Hugh said 'That went very well.' He imagined that the two cartons of fruit juice had gone round and, of course, knew nothing of Roberta's supplies. As I left to go back to England, he said 'I will miss John dreadfully but, please, never think of me as lonely. I will manage very well.' And he did.

19

As I flew home, I was apprehensive about the future. Our trio of friendship had been perfect and largely encouraged by John who had always had the greater need for outside life. Hugh seemed to be self-sufficient and I feared he might find it a strain to be alone with anyone – me, naturally, included. I need not have been anxious. We rang each other very often.

For many years we had an old fashioned neighbour in England who nursed a horror of homosexuality. If he thought he had spotted anyone with such tendencies (he was often mistaken), he always said 'I stood with my back to the wall the whole time the feller was in the room.' I told Hugh about him and he was much amused. From then on he would often start a telephone call with 'and HOW is back-to-the-wall?'

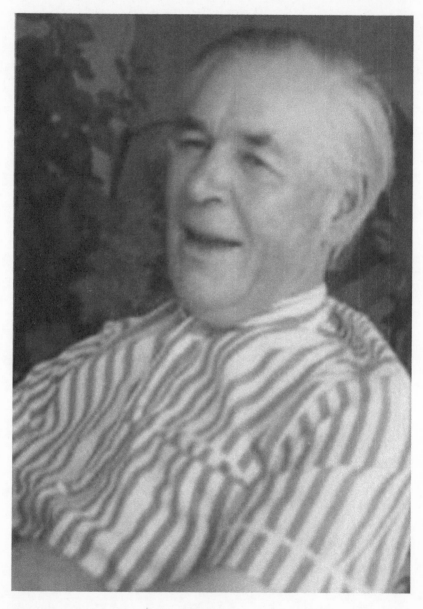

Hugh, 2000

Hugh, who had spent so many years trying to keep John in check used to frown, slightly, on 'fun.' Without John and his tendency to flirt and to flare up (particularly with bank managers, publishers and literary agents), Hugh, it seemed to me, began to allow the frivolous side of life to emerge. Not that he didn't miss John terribly.

John and Hugh had done more than well to make Valter their heir for, from then on, Valter assumed the role of Hugh's son. He guided him through complicated legal matters; saw to John's memorial stone and generally made certain that things were all right. He and Carl also treated me as a sister – perhaps an aunt for they were far younger than me. They always kept me up to date with Hugh's health and well being.

By December that year, I began to fret over Hugh's solitary Christmas. Carl and Valter always had to spend the festival with their own ageing parents.

John and Hugh had never gone in for balloons or crackers but Hugh always did buy a turkey at the supermarket and enjoyed concocting a complicated stuffing. I asked him what he planned to do, now alone, on that festive day. 'Nothing. I suppose. Just be Scrooge-like.'

I suggested sending him a parcel – as for troops in war time. At Partridges, in the Kings Road, they sold miniature Christmas cakes, plum puddings, small pots of brandy butter and packets of mince-pies – light as feathers. Hugh said 'Well. That would be very nice but NOT mince pies. I prefer my own pastry. I have, though, run out of mince meat.' Mince meat was only to be found in large, glass jars that were not easy to pack. Masses of bubble wrap and padding. Hugh was pleased and rang me when my first Christmas parcel arrived. 'I am about to roll the pastry and Leonie is eagerly awaiting the trimmings.' Leonie, a stray kitten, had replaced Timmy who died very soon after John's funeral.

Hugh began to return to outside life and often visited London, no longer by car, where he stayed in comfort at Durrant's Hotel and scoured the city for restaurants that still permitted smoking. The Poissonerie in Chelsea became the favourite. It ceased to exist in 2015 after running for fifty three years.

I nipped out to stay with Hugh whenever possible although the villa became more and more uncomfortable. Wiring was outlandish – plugs fell in tangled heaps from the wall and bed side lamps gave out blue flashes. I always tried to remember to take a strong torch with me. The small, stained bath took nearly an hour to fill – but only the hot (extremely hot) tap worked. I had to leave the water to cool down before getting in and, as I lay there, in the bath, paint flaked from the ceiling onto my face. Tiles were loose and dangerous to walk on. Lucia, talking non-stop, would bring me breakfast in bed. A hard circle of toast, strong cold coffee and an unripe fig. Hugh had lost the will to oversee. But we had fun. For supper one evening he prepared potted trout but was disappointed as he had not been able to find, in his view, all-important mace. The pudding he had cooked as an experiment. 'NOT one that I plan to repeat.' It was a sort of runny custard – but I liked it. We talked of many things. I remember, in particular, how Hugh had been shocked by aspects of Jim Lees Milne's diaries – especially a bit about Alvilde steaming open his letter 'Really disgraceful.' I took to popping to and fro to La Cavina for baths and comfort.

Hugh was always horrified when strangers rang in the hope of meeting him. Two newcomers to the district had been given an

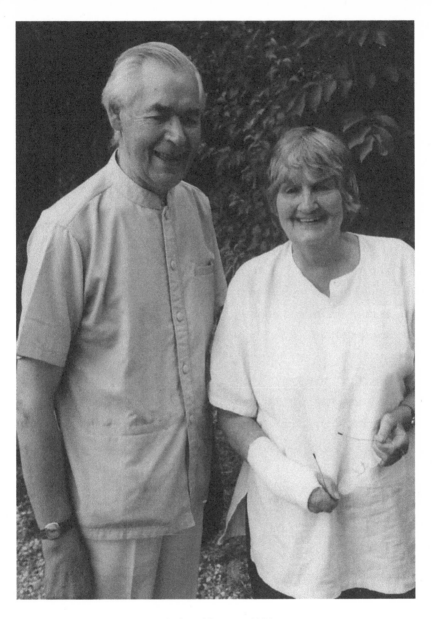

Hugh and Susanna, 2004

introduction 'by someone I don't care for. They want to come and see me. Why on earth?' I was back at La Cavina when he rang to say 'heaven knows why. I found myself inviting them both to lunch. A male couple.' He wanted me to meet them 'so we can decide, together, if they pass muster.' It was hot and heavy but windy too. A Hoopoe flew across the bonnet of my car as I rounded the bend to the Villa Marchio. Hugh had a laid a table out of doors – just by the lower entrance to the villa. The guests were late which made Hugh very nervous as he was concocting a cheese soufflé. I don't think the male couple can have passed muster as we never saw either of them again.

One morning, when I stayed there, the local priest arrived unexpectedly. He said he had come to bless the house. We were in the large sitting room and unprepared for him to pull a spray can from his pocket. He pressed the nozzle and squirted the room with holy water. Hugh did not especially like the priest or the squirting and said, very emphatically, 'I hope that has, at least, dealt with the mosquitoes.' Later, in the garden I admired the crocuses. He was extremely indignant 'They are NOT crocuses but Sternbergia.' It was misty that day and the view was lost to us but Hugh said 'I love the mist. It reminds me of Chinese pen and ink drawings.' He was a courageous person and always managed to find something to his taste, in spite of sadness, as the seasons changed.

I had many grandchildren and Hugh loved to hear of, as well as to see them. They too were out there a lot. When, some time later, my grandson, Bertram, was given his first car Hugh asked me to quote to him the words of his own mother as she handed him the keys to a Morris Minor. 'You are now in charge of a lethal weapon.' He often spoke of his mother who must have been a wise woman.

He never mentioned his father. We always talked of John and invariably said 'Great Scott, Good Grief and Mercy' to each other. Oddly, Hugh lost any interest in listening to music and he said 'reading is what I like best.'

In 2005, I badgered him again. I was getting an anthology together. It was called *Late Youth* and included the views of those who were getting older.

Hugh wrote the following piece

Inimitably, he called it 'Looking Forward'.

'Looking forward keeps me going. I clutch at the unconquerable hope that the book on which I am working will be better, at least more satisfying to me, than anything I have previously written and allow me time to begin another long meditated project. I look forward to the arrival of old and new books I have ordered and of periodicals – including the *Weekly Guardian*, which invites readers to 'share good news' although no paper makes a greater speciality of bad news. Out of doors, the expectation that plants in the little jungle that surrounds me will continue to overgrow – dispels the sadness of changing seasons.'

'Although I had a happy childhood, my main ambition was to grow up. When taken to a performance of Peter Pan, I was utterly mystified, as many other normal children must have been. I wanted to be allowed to stay up late. Soon I was asking for long trousers, conceded if only as armour against paedophiles. (Old men who wear shorts and unwittingly make themselves look still older merit a psychological study.)'

'Shaving was another fulfilled ambition still enjoyed as a morning ritual. And then driving a car; taking charge of a lethal weapon, as my mother told me.'

'"Youth's a stuff will not endure" – and a good thing too, I began to think. The youthful appearance I retained was a handicap when I began to write reviews of art exhibitions for *The Times* as a 'correspondent', a 'special correspondent' and finally 'our special correspondent' but without a name. Functionaries eyed me suspiciously as the representative of a paper that was still internationally respected. I longed for grey hairs, if not quite as many as I have today.'

'For fifty years I lived and worked with a companion who was perceived to be older than I was, though the age gap of no more than eight years became decreasingly significant and seemed to close. At home, he was addressed as '*Signor* Fleming' and I, as I still am, as *Signorino* ('master' – in the English usage of my childhood). In my professional world, however, I am treated with the deference accorded to age in Italy and have difficulty in persuading young colleagues to address me familiarly and by my Christian name as 'one of the boys' although I do not dye my hair or wear short trousers.'

'Never celebrating my birthday, I thought little about how old I was until recently when deteriorating eyesight made me acutely aware of advancing age, and an operation for cataract was recommended. "Don't have it," Viviana shrieked across a dinner table, "It's a terrible *shockkk*." I did and it was. When I took off the bandage next morning, the lined, grazed and haggard face that scowled back at me from the mirror was at least twenty years older than I had supposed it to be. As I went through the house, I saw cracks in the walls, scratches on the window panes, stains on upholstery, tarnish on the silver but also colours brighter than I had ever registered in works of art, exquisite details that I had forgotten.'

'Everyone that I met seemed to have put on twenty years since the previous day. So I wonder if I am not seeing myself as others see me, or whether they continue to see me as indistinctly as I had previously seen them. I overhears someone say of me "he's seventy seven but doesn't look a day over sixty-nine." Apparently I do not pass muster to attract gerontophiles but there is still hope for the future.'

I stayed again at the tumble-down villa. Hugh was low but it was heaven to see him and he was pleased with the double-edged razor blades, stem ginger and chocolates I handed him. We had many laughs about the people he can no longer cope with. 'A fair number. One of them tries to help in an annoying way; stacking and rinsing the plates. Quite unnecessary.'

Hugh told me of his accountant wanting to borrow a huge sum of money. 'It was very awkward as, being my accountant, he knew I could lend it.' Later, the accountant (who was never able to repay him) took him two pots of honey. 'The most expensive honey I've ever had.'

I noted that Hugh had large, dark patches on his arms. He said 'I daresay it's the Black Death.' His back was very bent and I suggested trying to stand straight for a few minutes every day. He said 'I wouldn't dream of it.'

I was happy to be there but got stuck in my bedroom for over an hour as the door had warped.

20

Hugh, in Indian white, pointed to Leonie – now fully grown 'Quite beguiling' he said 'but she'll never be as pretty as Timmy.' I wasn't sure. Timmy rather lost her looks towards the end and John turned against her when he was ill.

Champagne on the loggia. Hugh managed to ration me by stopping the bottle with a gadget that I'd bought for him at Peter Jones. Dreadful drought in Italy but his water was just holding out. He had lately read a book by an archaeologist he knew – on Alfred Maudslay and said it was interesting but badly written. Full of screech marks. 'I'd expected the exact reverse – well written but boring.'

We both, after two years, found it hard to believe that John was not with us in his chef's trousers. We drank tea from the tarnished silver tea-pot left to him by Father Charles, head of the Brompton Oratory (whose cell there had been decorated by David Hicks).

We had been asked to a glittering and international dinner at the Villa Reale. Hugh was dressed in white and we set off together. We finally gained entry to the park after some misunderstanding with a grumpy and unwilling guard at the lodge. He had thought we were impostors. Statues surrounding the villa had all been cleaned and looked bright, white and new. 'They look simply ghastly', Hugh said. Waiters galore served us at a table below the front steps. Hugh much enjoyed it. 'Like something in an old film.' Viviana, one of the ageing Pecci Blunt daughters, could never sit still. She kept getting up from the table and roaming around – like a child. Her masterful older sister, Letizia, dressy and bejewelled, became furious with her – shouting 'You only ever think of yourself.' Camilla, ravishingly beautiful behind a zimmer frame, beamed and photographed every second of the goings on.

Hugh, although still able to be amused by the odd outing, was, at that time, puzzled by his own lack of strength and was given daily injections in the stomach by Lucia 'who does it badly.'

One afternoon we walked together to the cottages where a children's party raged in the heat. A mountain of profiteroles melted in the sun beside a birthday cake decorated in dripping chocolate. Brown-legged children screamed and fought in an inflatable pool. Hugh said how thankful he was not to be a paedophile, 'those children in the pool would have been very tempting to one.' He added, 'of course I now realise that I was regularly interfered with when at school. I didn't mind a scrap and never felt it was worth mentioning to my mother.'

Soon after that I realised that I had reached the pinnacle of social ambition when Hugh drove me, many kilometres, to a party thrown by Muriel Spark to celebrate the seventieth birthday of her companion in life, the sculptress, Penelope Jardine. We had been warned that Dame Muriel entertained on a shoe string; that her wine tasted as though it came from a car exhaust and that rats tended to nibble at one's shoes. We were both apprehensive though much enjoyed the drive – Hugh smoked all the way. But no. It was done in tune to one of Muriel's novels – sheer surprise. We parked in an olive grove from which candles, in glass holders, guided us to vast tents – waiters in white coats, champagne in pewter buckets and unimaginably luscious 'starters' – a meal in themselves. There were about a hundred guests – few of whom we knew. Lots from Edinburgh. Muriel lively and colourfully dressed. Penelope sweet and friendly (I had just overlapped with her at boarding school). Later we were all seated for supper – no trace of a rat – and treated to at least eight courses. After the first five, we were served slices of water-melon to 'cleanse the palate' before the next three came on. Hugh decided to pretend to think that water-melon heralded the end and signalled to me – so we left very early. Few but Hugh would have thought it possible to do that. In the car he gave way to one of his few (in my presence) misogynistic moments. 'It was all very well for you. You sat next to clever men but I got the wives.'

That outing took place shortly before the invasion of Iraq. Hugh loathed both Bush and Blair. He said, as he drove and smoked, 'their eyes get closer and closer together every time I see them on television and, by the way, I am absolutely certain that there are no weapons of mass destruction in Iraq.'

A little later that year, my ageing uncle, Robin Chancellor, alone in his Northamptonshire pavilion, began to yearn for a companion.

He surfed the net and believed that he might have found happiness on a sex-condominium outside Bangkok. Off he toiled to meet his 'date' – a Thai grandfather called Prim. Prim, as it turned out, after a brief experiment, refused to share the only bed in the bungalow with Uncle Robin on account, he said, of Robin's loud snoring. He, himself, had to sleep under the table in the kitchen. Uncle Robin fully believed it to be only a question of snoring. He had fallen for Prim and planned to go home but to return to the sex-condominium as soon as he could find a cure.

Naturally I told Hugh the whole story and he promised to try and help. A week later he rang me to say that he'd seen an advertisement for a snoring cure on the back of the gardening catalogue which supplied his favourite light reading. He couldn't, though, order it until he was ready for more Tomorite and a new watering can. That way he would get free delivery.

Eventually a small parcel arrived at my house in England – addressed in Hugh's hand. Inside the message read 'I hope this will help with Uncle Robin's predicament.'

My twelve-year-old grandson, Bertram, was with me (on an exeat from school) when the package came and he was very useful in helping me to assemble the contraption. It had to be clamped to the nose. My grandson doubled up when I told him what it was for; his great, great uncle's sex life.

Unfortunately it turned out, on my uncle's next visit to Thailand, that it was not only the snoring that Prim objected to – in spite of Uncle Robin having hopefully plugged himself into the device.

Hugh was vastly amused by the whole topic.

By then I had become a good friend of Sarah Riddell. Hugh had

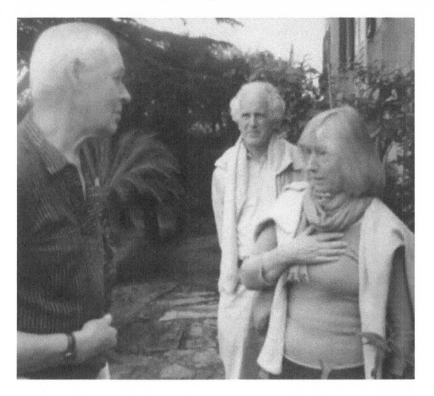

Hugh, John Riddell, and Sarah Riddell, 2007

always much hoped to see her again one day but it was beyond him to have guests apart from his extended (not very extended) family. Nicky and I asked the Riddells to stay with us in Italy, mainly because we much enjoyed their company and partly so that I could bring Sarah and Hugh together again. They had barely met since the John Calmann days. I took John and Sarah to the Villa Marchio where we found Hugh tottering on the path by the growth-entangled gate. He had forgotten we were coming and looked stunned. Such things were beginning to happen to his memory. He recovered very quickly in his joy at seeing Sarah again. In no time

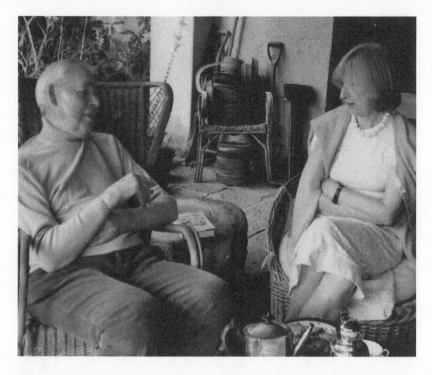

Hugh with Sarah

they were reliving the old days. He loved it and gave Sarah a copy of the eighth edition of their joint enterprise. He did, to my surprise, allow John Riddell to help him with the tea-tray. He had never let me do that. Maybe it was 'men only.'

He complained that the cigarettes brought to him at great expense by some no-longer-approved-of friend, were 'disgusting.'

Not long after that, when we were back in England, Valter rang to tell us that Hugh was in hospital having had a stroke. He had fallen in the garden but had crawled in doors to the telephone to ring Dr Nottoli – who drove him straight to the hospital in Pescia. Poor Hugh suffered from nicotine withdrawal there.

154

When he got home I went to stay with him for a few days. He was very set in his ways and resented being unable to go to the supermarket for a while. 'Lucia is hopeless at shopping. If I ask for a trout and there isn't one – she doesn't know what to get instead.'

The oil tank was empty and it was extremely cold.

A little later Nicky and I both went to see him. He greeted us in a bright green polo-necked sweater given to him by Valter. He was slow and shuffly. He told us of his ambulance drive to Pescia where he supposed he was going to die.

He said 'I thought that's OK because Zanna will come to see me 'laid out' and will finally be able to get to visit the Deposizione which she's always longed to see.' Very trusting of him (he knew that it had always been impossible, up until then, for me to track down anyone with a key to the chapel where the Deposizione was on display). He carried the tea-tray and held it at such an angle that it spilled until the tea-pot was empty. He was weak but laughed until tears fell. He walked with us, lurching through overgrowth, to the gate which was entangled in a vast lime tree – to the extent that it could neither be opened nor closed. I mumbled a snatch of the Kipling poem to myself.

> They shut the road through the woods
> Seventy years ago '
> Weather and rain have undone it again
> And now you would never know
> There once was a road through the woods

We said goodbye as a thunder storm threatened.

Later that year Thekla rang to say 'Isn't it wonderful about

Hugh's honour.' At first I thought she said 'Hugh Honour.' I had heard nothing of it although I spoke to Hugh at least twice a week. He said, 'Thekla is very generous. It's only something from Bassano University. I didn't think it worth mentioning. I've got to go there and I'm simply dreading it.' After the event he rang me to say that it had been hellish. He'd had to sit on a stage in a large theatre with the Mayor and corporation and then to give a discourse in Italian. The only saving grace, though, was that he had, with difficulty, managed to prevent anyone he knew from attending.

He described how Leonie had got her teeth into Lucia who had to be given endless injections and bled all over the kitchen. Hugh was on Leonie's side.

One evening he told me, by telephone, that he had choked badly on dry toast and chicken liver. He wouldn't eat goose liver any more – too cruel – the geese being stuffed. He had become very fond of his own gaggle.

On one of my holidays in our Lucchese house Hugh rang and begged me to go over to help with some Americans – to *'tenere banco'* (Roberta's expression for keeping a conversation going.) There were four of them – ardent admirers of John and Hugh and they weren't easy to chase away. They kept asking Hugh for directions, by road, to Rome and Hugh kept saying 'I haven't the faintest idea.'

When they'd gone he said, 'thank God that's over.

He then told me a story he'd just heard by telephone from Michael Mallon. Givenchy had thrown a party for Jayne Wrightsman in Paris and provided all the Louis XVIII furniture himself – except for round tables that hadn't existed at that date. He'd had them made especially. Jayne Wrightsman chucked the same day.

156

I stayed for supper which Hugh cooked with difficulty. He wore his green jumper but, apart from poor gait, was in great heart. He had been both puzzled and amused when he heard a young hanger-on, who was there for a day or two, saying on his mobile telephone 'I'm staying with my old guardian near Lucca.' Hugh said 'that merits many screech marks. What can he have meant?' That particular guest had given his 'guardian' a copy of a novel called *The Kindly Ones* – about Nazi atrocities. Hundreds of pages of scatological horror. It made Hugh depressed for weeks but he always felt that he had to finish a book once he'd started it.

He also said that Valter had given him two beautiful walking sticks but that he wasn't going to use them.

When I got back to England he told me that he was low and depressed. I implored him to stop reading that dreadful book. He'd been miserable ever since he started it. He wouldn't take my advice but did, eventually, finish it and immediately cheered up.

21

It was when Hugh turned eighty that things started to go really wrong. He, although reluctant to celebrate even a milestone birthday, had been persuaded to dine at Cecco's in Pescia. It was his favourite local restaurant. He was much loved there and they allowed him, but only him, to smoke. Friends from Florence were with him but I was unable to go. The next day I learnt that he had, in the middle of dinner, had a black-out and had fallen onto the hard, tiled floor.

From there he was removed to the familiar hospital in Pescia. I went to see him soon after he got home. He said 'Once again I thought about you coming to see me 'laid out' and also to see the Deposizione.' He was tottery but brushed his health aside by quoting from one of Muriel Spark's novels 'I cannot abide people to be off colour.'

On that visit I was more than ever struck by the dilapidated state of the house. On the way to the loggia – in the angle of the main block and the smaller wing – there was a crack so wide I could have put my arm into it. It was during a dry summer month and the *Dahlia Imperialis* grew to the height of the upper floor window sill. The loggia, no more than a simple lean-to with a pillar at each corner and a door leading to the back garden – was tumbling down. One of the main beams that supported the roof was cracked and the building had begun to subside. It looked near to caving in.

Whilst I was there my teenage grandson, Bertram, visited us – he was staying in 'our' house – which for many years had belonged to our daughter, Clara – Bertram's mother. He was alive to the wonders of the Villa Marchio and the 'awesome' presence of Hugh. His generation had, of course, all heard of Honour and Fleming – had been made to read their books at school. He was amazed that his rather scatty grandmother should have such a distinguished friend. He stared and said 'Gosh Lola (filippino for grandmother). This is marvellous – a real time warp' – as he noted the old Olivetti typewriter, brimming ash-trays, dangling curtains, cracks in walls and chipped, floating tiles.

Time warp? Strange for me as I reached back in my head to the freshness of that day when I first went there with John and Hugh – before they had moved in.

Hugh began to fall more and more often. Not black-outs but bad tumbles. He often rang me and, one evening, told me, humorously, that he had fallen during the night and cracked a rib. Small wonder. The brick-work in his bedroom was hazardous. He had lain on his back for five hours – unable to move. I asked, 'what on earth did you think about when you were on your back for so long?' He answered 'I just thought about how to get up.'

I suggested having a carpet laid in his bedroom but he said 'No. Bricks look so much nicer.'

Once, on my arrival, he told me an awful story. 'I was followed to the house by a man outside the supermarket. He trailed behind me in the car. When we got out he said he was delivering watches. As soon as he saw the puny Luigi he scuttled. I expect he was a drug dealer.' It was agony to think of Hugh living alone and barely able to walk. God knows how he managed to drive and shop. 'At least', he said, 'I wasn't coshed – although, I'm told, that when Diana Cooper was gagged and bound, she thoroughly enjoyed it.'

Whatever Hugh's condition, he never failed to ask me what I was reading. I had become obsessed with Meredith and told him that I was re-reading *The Egoist*. He said, very simply and spontaneously 'the dainty rogue in porcelain.' What a memory – out of the blue and a book he hadn't read for forty years or more. 'And' he added 'of course he had a leg.'

One day, as I bumped down Hugh's road, I saw the damage done to his olives and cypresses (he had told me of a fire there). Hugh was older and stiffer but, otherwise unchanged. He was funny, not in the least bit deaf and, since the cataract, clear-sighted. Between us, it took an age to carry the bottle and glasses to the loggia. I broke a glass. The evening was lovely. Crescent moon. A mouse in a trap and long dead, was hurtled about by Leonie. She looked better in her winter coat – dreadfully scrawny in summer.

Tomato soup, hot-pot and stewed pears for supper. Hugh took a long time, refusing help, fetching food from the kitchen in near darkness. Wit sharper than ever and a plan for the following day. He liked to talk about his visits to the supermarket. They had

161

always held excitement for him and, with his outside life shrinking, they were becoming more and more important.

The next day we went to lunch at the Villa Reale. Me driving. For ten minutes after our arrival we found no one. Camilla eventually emerged on a zimmer frame, beautiful but almost invisible having had a stroke and a broken leg. We waited under a huge magnolia. Waited and waited. Camilla called 'Emiliano' loud and often but no one came. 'He's the butler' she explained 'and I loathe him. He's only temporary but has fallen in love with a Chinese boy who has been helping in the kitchen for the summer. He drove him to Pisa this morning. Probably threw himself onto the track.'

Emiliano appeared in the end – to be cross-questioned and insulted by Camilla. He brought a fancy feast to the garden (Hugh revelling in it all) and set it under the shade of the enormous magnolia. Camilla had had a boring summer with her sister driving her mad. Letizia had taken two sleeping pills instead of a half and had fallen out of bed. She had lain on the floor for most of the night. Hugh told us a story about an Anglo-Tuscan lion-huntress who had cornered him at a party, many years back, and asked impertinent questions about me. He and John had refused ever to see her again in spite of her constant beseeching for permission to visit. 'Wonderful to have had an excuse', Hugh said. I was puzzled never to have heard that story before but Hugh explained, 'we didn't like to tell you at the time. John said you would have been so cross with the lady in question.'

After lunch we set off, with tremendous difficulty, for Pescia – the furious and love-lorn Emiliano driving. Camilla had a basket attached to her zimmer in which she carried a clanking camera. We had difficulty in finding the tiny chapel that had eluded me for so long. It was opposite the hospital where Hugh had expected me to come and see him laid-out and where patients walked about in their dressing gowns – smoking. The chapel was shut and I was sure that I was doomed never to see inside it. Hugh remained doggedly optimistic as a face appeared through a grid and the owner of the face told us that the key was to be found in the hospital where the priests worked. We had a very long wait with Camilla almost doubled up and Hugh supported by the unpopular Emiliano. Finally there we were – in the tiny chapel with the perfect wooden carving before our eyes – faded in colour but beautifully restored. Hugh told us that his last visit there had been with two keen art historians. There had been an open coffin in the aisle with women kneeling beside it – 'rather disconcerting.' Suddenly there was a violent screeching. Hugh thought the women had all gone mad but it turned out that one of his companions had set off the alarm by trying to get a closer look.

Back at the Villa Reale, Emiliano reluctantly brought us tea on the lawn. Camilla said that she had been worn out by her sister, Letizia, constantly persuading famous people to stay at the Villa during the summer. Hugh sympathised and said how awful it was having to meet celebrities. When he was a boy, his aunt had rented a house in Frinton where they saw a man with a beard. His aunt hissed 'I think that is Bernard Shaw.' The old man removed his hat and said 'yes, I am.'

22

Hugh fell more often and, as time passed, his legs weakened more and more. Neither the loyal Dr Nottoli nor any of his colleagues could find an explanation. Hugh was enjoying collaborating with Paolo Mariuz, an erudite scholar from Bassano, with his work on Canova who, Hugh told me 'was a VERY nice man.' Domestically, though, he was struggling. Valter organised a physiotherapist to try to help strengthen Hugh's legs but Hugh didn't take to him – said his eyes were too far apart. He fell frequently – often spending hours on his back. But he steadfastly refused to have anyone to live in the house. He also refused to move to a ground floor bedroom. There were forty steps between his bedroom and the basement kitchen – each one hard and chipped. Friends still loved to be in Hugh's company and many visited in that remote spot. Thekla

Clark, Nicholas and Mary Penny, Fausto Calderai, Neri Torrigiani, Penelope Jardine, Dimitri Zikos, David Plante and Jonathan Burnham. Thekla, indeed, telephoned him most evenings at six o'clock on the dot. Carl and Valter were there whenever needed. I stayed often and wished that Hugh wouldn't continue to cook elaborate meals – carrying food and dishes from the kitchen to the dining room on wobbly legs; soup spilling and serving spoons clattering to the ground. Each course was a frightful effort. Once he set a frying pan on fire. He was again driving himself to the supermarket, lurching round the aisles with a trolley and, more than once, falling in the car park. One day (and not a day too soon) his driving licence was removed when he went to renew it. It was an appalling moment. Driving had always been Hugh's favourite sport. Some 'bitch' at the local council had watched from a window as he struggled across the yard and straight away, no questions asked, had put a firm 'NO' on his application form.

Valter had the excellent idea of converting the barn below the house, He and Carl were prepared to move there and to keep an eye on Hugh. They asked me to put the suggestion to him. They felt that, if he objected, he would not like to tell them face to face. On my very next visit, I brought the subject up. Hugh looked disconcerted and said 'but WHERE would Lucia hang out the washing?' He had become resistant to any form of change.

His wits were never diminished however. Once I rang him to complain about a rabbit eating my lettuces. I could see one doing it from my window. Without a pause he said,

> The rabbit has a charming face
> It's private life is a disgrace

I really dare not say to you
The awful things that rabbits do
They have such lost, degraded souls
No wonder that they live in holes.
When such depravity is found
It only can live underground.

At first I thought he was just chatting – but no. The entire rhyme came straight out of his memory.

He began to sleep more during the day – sitting in John's old study, bulging pictures of male nudes on the walls. Chain smoking – sometimes with nearly an inch of burnt out tobacco at the end of his cigarette. Ash all over his clothes – particularly as his hands weakened. In many ways, though, he was his old self.

Sometimes he became muddled. One day he rang me and asked 'why don't you come to tea with me every day like you used to?' I had to reply 'because I live in Oxfordshire.'

'More to the point, then, when are you coming out?'

On one or two occasions, when I rang him, he dropped the telephone mid-sentence and all I could hear were his groans as he struggled to pick it up from the floor.

Once he rang sounding shaken, to say he had woken in the night to see, just discernible by moonlight, the dark, slight figure of a youth who slowly helped himself to all pocketable things in the room – china, hair brushes, silver-framed photographs. Even something almost touching the pillow on which Hugh feigned sleep, was silently removed. He said 'I thought it wise to stay quite still with my eyes closed.' In the morning he found that two thousand Euros had been taken from a drawer. The intruder had also eaten his way through a piece of ham and the remains of a trout. 'I keep thinking how lucky he was', Hugh said. He seemed to be resigned and almost defeated by everything. We all worried that he had become easy prey – alone and falling constantly at the villa.

One more fall triggered the necessity of Valter finding a 'carer.' When it was put to him Hugh said 'Very well then. But it must be a man, very good looking and absolutely silent.'

23

In December 2011 Valter found, almost miraculously, the handsome and silent Saman (curiously a diminutive of Samantha). He was from Sri Lanka and had been working as a *badante* in Naples – sending money home to his wife, Dulit and his small son, Asala. He got the hang of the job in an instant. He set up a small gingham-cloth-covered dining table that looked like a Mary Fedden picture in John's study and bathed and shaved Hugh. Hugh's condition had worsened and Saman drove, shopped and almost carried Hugh up and down the perilous stairs. Hugh still refused to change bedrooms. 'No. If I leave my room I might never go upstairs again.' Much as Hugh liked Saman he was unnerved by the changes in his way of life and couldn't help complaining 'His food is dreary and he shops extravagantly – also he won't allow me to

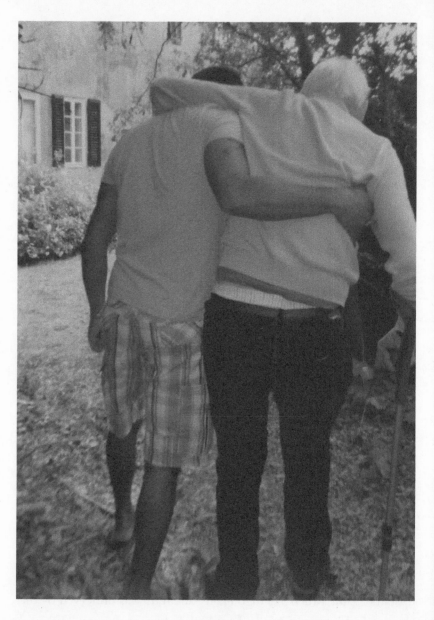

Hugh with Saman

walk on my own which is irritating.' Saman was long suffering and didn't complain about cooking in the grim bogey-hole of a kitchen. It was dangerous with trailing pipes and leaking gas.

With the anxiety of Hugh falling or burning the house down – now allayed, I was able to enjoy staying there again in spite of the discomfort. Radiators were rusty brown and, mostly, no longer in use. Saman was perfect for the job. He cooked and carried meal after meal to the newly-invented dining room table and, although it struck me as delicious, Hugh never conceded that he cooked well. 'Rather Sri Lankan', he would say after Saman had heaved him, jolting and shuddering, to the table. Very importantly, Lucia took to Saman. She was an integral part of the household, had worked there for many years and doted on Hugh; still calling him *Signorino* notwithstanding his white hair and withered limbs.

After a bit of time, Hugh managed to stop fretting about domestic matters and admitted he 'much enjoyed' being washed and shaved each day by this strikingly handsome young man.

We used to talk about John, the Sutros, Freya Stark, Lerici, Hugh's mother, books, Canova and almost everything else. Saman was happy to drive me into Lucca – to drop me outside the walls for a few hours and to fetch me again in time for lunch.

One afternoon my dear neighbour, Jenny Brewer came to tea bringing her friend, Massimo Malatesta (an art historian) with her. Once Jenny had mentioned Hugh's name to him and he had been aghast. 'Not THE Hugh Honour?' He had no idea that Hugh lived in the neighbourhood. They were happy to meet but Hugh was happier still when Massimo rescued a hedgehog from the lotus pond that was being restored on Valter's instructions. With Saman behind the wheel chair, it would now be possible for Hugh to get

171

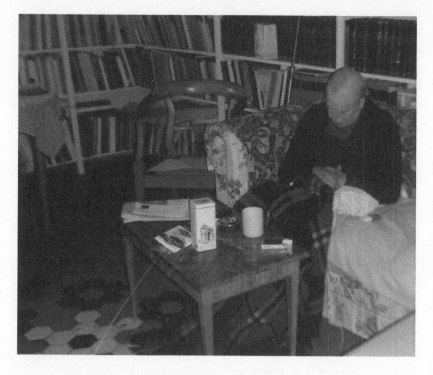

Hugh in his study, asleep

to the loggia and from there to gaze at the pond and hear the frogs again. It had leaked and dried up and the hedgehog had fallen into the empty cistern. Massimo brought the hedgehog in to visit Hugh who was vastly touched and entertained.

Hugh was sweet and smiling. He could no longer write – his hands had lost their strength – but could, just, reach for a cigarette and, after several attempts, light it. Flaming matches fell to the floor. I walked round the garden and picked two black tulips to put in a pot on the supper table. Neither of us were able to open the chocolate box. Hugh was determined to try – using an army knife with feeble fingers. I had to call Saman. I was pleased to be there –

owls hooted and a mad cat outside my bedroom window gave me weird glances with spooky eyes. Leone had been joined by yet another cat called Cleopatra. She was horrible and kept climbing on to my bed and clawing at my paper thin skin. I tried hypnotising her to no effect.

Saman showed me many pictures of his small dark son and his pretty wife. Valter had begun complicated arrangements for them to be brought over to join Saman at the Villa Marchio.

24

In 2014, Dulit and Asala arrived to join Saman. Hugh, never before a child-lover, adored the little boy. He was only two but quiet and well mannered. Hugh refused to learn his name and insisted on calling him Antonio. It was odd to have the house so child-dominated – toys everywhere and much giggling as 'Antonio' ran in and out of John's study. He often kissed Hugh on the lips and Hugh was delighted.

Of course, too, Hugh's days could be long and dull. If he tried to read he would instantly fall asleep or just loll, half awake, on the collapsing sofa watching crazy television advertisements and scraps of violent news.

His mind sometimes became muddled. Valter always kept me up to date. Telephoning directly to Hugh had become a problem but,

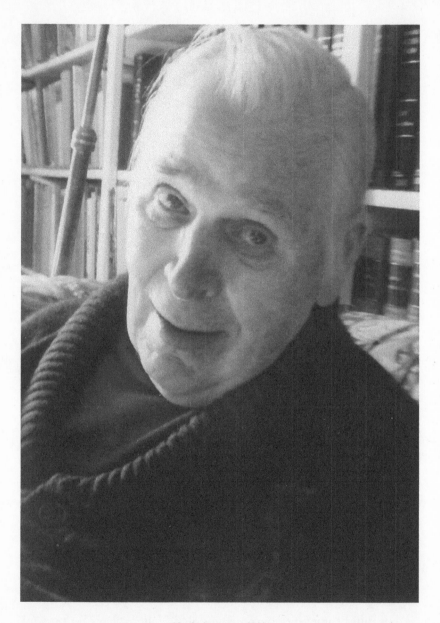

Hugh, last snap 2015

occasionally we managed a chat. Once he said 'I drove to meet you at Pescia station but you weren't there. A VERY nice man asked me to go back with him for supper. He gave me a simply delicious meal.' I found it touching and consistent with Hugh's character that his imaginary outing should have ended happily.

Saman monitored Hugh's smoking – only permitting it when somebody was present. He did, though, begin to worry about carrying Hugh up to bed – and down again each morning. Hugh was tall and heavy – a dead weight. No life in his limbs. One day when I was there I decided to become bossy. What if Saman put his back out? Valter always hesitated before making changes on Hugh's behalf for fear of causing him distress. With Valter's full permission (and strong hope that the plan would succeed) I called the ever faithful Dr Notolli who immediately banned the stairs and Hugh was moved to the ground floor – to a pretty room – 'my' room, that looked out, from one window, to the cedar tree and from the other – to the hills. The room was lined with travel books and Hugh's favourite old tweed coat bulged through a William Morris cupboard curtain.

On one wall hung a small, cracked oil painting of an orchestra – local to Berwick-on-Tweed – where John and Hugh had, a very long time before, found it in a junk shop. Although initially fearful of any form of change, Hugh tended to accept a *fait accompli* with resignation. 'I suppose it's inevitable.'

Little 'Antonio' brought much delight. Hugh told me 'He sits on my knee when I'm driving the car.' That, I'm afraid was wishful thinking – his not having driven for a long while by then. In spite of the question as to where Lucia was to hang out the washing, Carl and Valter started to restore the barn. They planned to live there and to be close at hand. Hugh was pleased and became fond of the builders who came from Naples and were very good looking.

I began to write him long letters, like a school girl, and Valter would read them aloud to him.

25

The last year or two of Hugh's life are hard to write, or even to think, about. Although he was released from domestic worries and happy to be surrounded by a cheery Sri Lankan family, the days were long and his body useless. He was pleased, though, to know that Saman was keeping the garden in check and that, too, he was putting a lot of energy into tending the olives. I was distressed by Hugh's pitch black feet. I told him to wiggle his toes a bit but he looked bored by the suggestion. He told me, when we were alone, that he was sometimes distressed by emotional thoughts and was spending sleepless nights. Tears came into his eyes. We went back to talking of John. Talking of John always seemed to calm him.

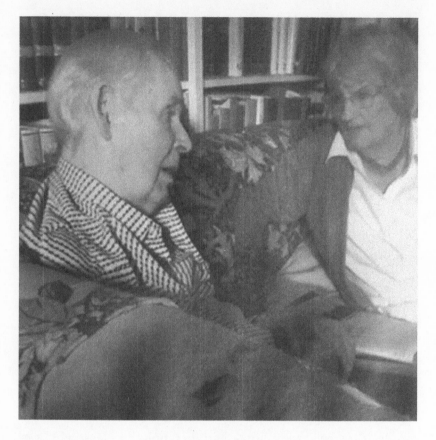

Saying goodbye

I had hit on an idea. It was this; when we were at La Cavina, we would only have friends to stay who wanted to see Hugh and who Hugh, in his turn, much hoped to see again. Sarah Riddell, Richard and Hatty Dorment, Selina Hastings, Claire Ward, Mary Christie, Tessa Baring and others. I had to rotate them carefully as, by now, a number of those friends could no longer get up to our top floor – the stairs being pretty steep.

In the summer of 2015 I had some perfect guests. Very sadly Sarah Riddell (his top treat) was unable to get to Italy in the end as she was suddenly ill, but all other visits were a vast success. Saman had wheeled Hugh into the big and beautiful main sitting room (the bookish atmosphere, once again, reminded me of Percy Lubbock and of our youthful years at Lerici) where he was placed on a sagging sofa. Richard (whom Hugh considered to be the best living art critic) talked to him about the museum world, Selina about every topic, Claire about gardening and the rest of us joined in.

Hugh was weak and could no longer walk at all – or even get much use out of his hands. With the help of Saman, though, he did manage the occasional cigarette and still loved the Charbonnel et Walker chocolates that I provided him with. They often melted before he ate them – then he would pour them into his mouth leaving trails of chocolate dripping down his shirt. As we sat with him there was very often a wistful and beguiling look in his eyes.

My visitors were all thrilled to see him but each felt that it was probably for the last time. And so it proved.

On my final day of that particular holiday, when our visitors had gone home, I went to the Villa Marchio with Nicky (who's walking too, was troublesome.) I had the idea, rather late in the day, of using Hugh's wheel chair to fetch him at the gate. It was great that the two were, thus, able to meet. We sat in the loggia. Saman had wheeled Hugh out there and we chatted with no reserve. It was what my mother used to call 'a well seasoned friendship.' As we left I said to

181

Hugh, 'All our visitors were so honoured (apt word to use) to see you here. You have so many ardent admirers that I'm rather ashamed to have always taken you for granted.'

He took my hand, gave a celestial smile and said – very firmly – 'I should hope so too.'

That was the last time I saw him. He died in May 2016 and was buried in the Tofori graveyard beside John. His death was followed by many glowing obituaries. He would have been horrified.

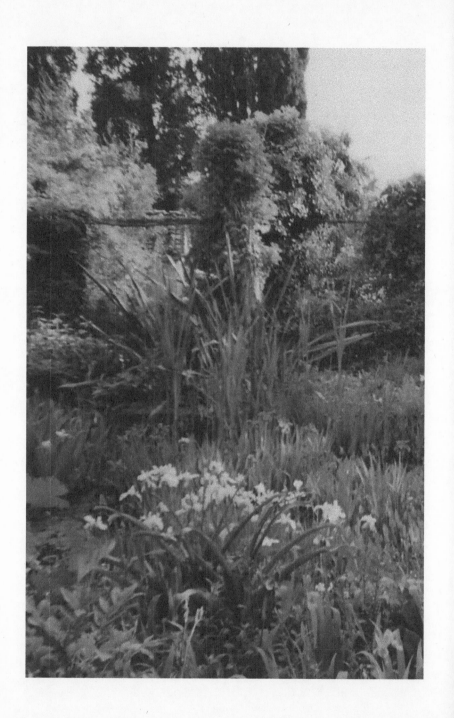

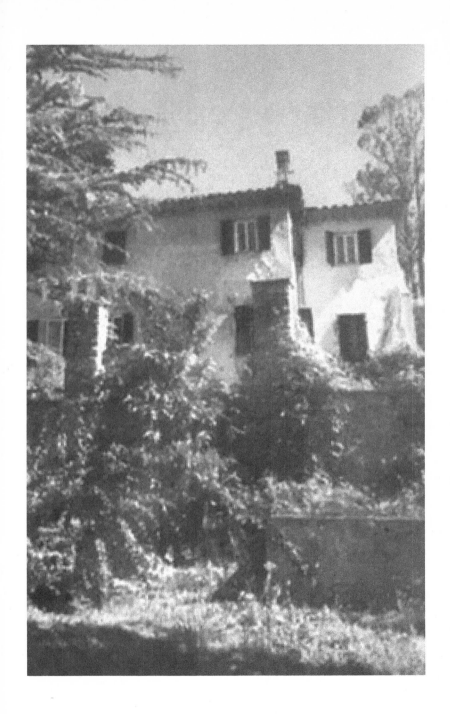

Postscripts

I asked my daughter, Clara Weatherall, to add her impressions to this memoir. John and Hugh had become members of our family and we were all involved. Or invOLved, as Hugh would have said.

My early memories of John and Hugh are of being told to behave and to be seen and not heard when they came to lunch. I remember my mother's warning. 'They are eminent art historians, experts in everything and they do not like children,' They were a daunting pair, perhaps more because of the build up than because they actually were. Their friendship with my parents was a very close one and I think, because of that, they actually made an effort to talk to us although they were never quite sure how to go about it!

As we grew up we were allowed to go with our parents to the Villa Marchio. It was and is a magical place. My mother was with them when they first found the house and they were all spell bound. The *piano nobile* was reached by walking up a double outside staircase, the hallmark of so many beautiful Italian villas. John and Hugh made it wonderful with a library full of extraordinary books – there were books everywhere.

Not surprisingly 'the boys' had a terrific eye and they bought very good Italian and English furniture. The villa was not grand but full of stimulating works of art and evidence that their erudition was overpowering. Copies of *TLS*, *Literary Review*, *Art Quarterly* and other literary magazines were strewn across tables and desks – burying typewriters and overflowing ashtrays.

We would sit outside under the loggia – built from a sketch by my father – and they would speak in their wonderful drawly way about their trips to London by car (Hugh did all the driving as John never had a licence) to buy marmite and to visit publishers.

When I married Percy my parents gave us the house we had spent our holidays in. I had always loved it there and had lived for a year or more in Italy so was pretty fluent in Italian. It was after that that I began to see more of John and Hugh. We loved to hear stories of their adventures in Syria and Jordan – Sicily, Greece and Turkey. Hugh in particular was very good at remembering every detail of the works of art they had seen. Their descriptions of Aleppo were especially poignant.

But they had their light side. They enjoyed gossip and were always intrigued by the endless complications of my mother's family and their mutual friends in England. John had developed a naughty glint – the result of his growing taste for Thai holidays – and I could see they enjoyed discovering life outside the art world.

Percy has a terrific memory and after John died – he and Hugh talked endlessly about art in an historical context.

Hugh started to grow old and infirm and his continual dread was never to be able to do things again.

One year it was 'I'll never be able to drive to London again.' The next 'I will never visit Rome again.' – 'I can't walk around Lucca again' and so on until he was no longer able to leave the house.

The boys had a particular foible. It became more and more dilapidated. Alarming cracks appeared in the walls and the electrics were death defying. The garden, so beautifully created by Hugh, fell into abandonment and in the end it was almost like working ones way through the forest in Beauty and the Beast to get to the house.

Percy and I continued to visit Hugh every time we were in Italy. The saggy sofas became even saggier, the carpets more threadbare and the windows more cracked. Even when Hugh was hardly able to speak and sometimes confused me with my mother – he was always able to engage. He became sad though – often telling me that he wanted to be 'gathered.'

Carl and Valter are as good friends to us as they were to John and Hugh – and are to my parents and my sisters. Some years ago, during Hugh's life time, it was decided that we enter into partnership with Valter when he took on the barn that Hugh had made over to him. One of the greatest moments was when

Hugh, accompanied by the marvellous Sri Lankan carer, Saman, came to a party on the building site to join the workers. It was a beautiful day in March and we were able to sit outside and break bread with the team who had worked so hard to restore the barn to glory and to create a state of the art home for Carl and Valter. Hugh wept with overflowing delight.

When Hugh died, Carl and Valter wanted to live in their newly converted barn and the opportunity came for us to take over the Villa Marchio. Restoration will constitute a huge project but Percy, myself and our four children love the house and its connection with our family.'

My second daughter Lily Pollock also remembers John and Hugh:

Many of my twenty or so birthdays were spent in our house in Italy, our home from home, just outside the beautiful walled city of Lucca. A great fuss was made. Exotic Italian presents were brought and there was always a party. Entering my teenage years – local boys were included on my guest list. Mum asked a few of her own friends for moral support. Two of them were always John and Hugh. I remember fearing that having 'grown-ups' at the party was going to be a bore. Of course John and Hugh were the life and soul. They brought with them a hint of magic. A beautiful bunch of flowers from their garden made me feel glamorous and they lavished attention on us all (particularly the local lads) with many a twinkle. It never occurred to either of them to talk to us on any level other than their own; ranging from the height of sophistication to the depths of outrageous humour. No guest was left unnoticed. Thanks to John and Hugh there was never any ice to be broken at my birthday parties – just a glass or two with the bonhomie and flowing wine.

Our youngest daughter Silvy Weatherall wrote of her memories. Thus our whole family is included in this memoir:

> Strawberries and cream
> Bangers and mash
> Fred and Ginger
> Art and Culture (think Trivial Pursuit)
> Cheese and wine
> Gilbert and George
> Kensington and Chelsea
> John and Hugh

When I was a child, staying at our house near Lucca for six weeks of every summer holiday, John and Hugh were a regular feature. Their names rolled off our tongues as one. They were a unit – virtually indistinguishable. As I grew older I was able to separate them by their physical attributes. They were never particularly good with young children so I generally observed from afar.

I don't think John could cook. He was scruffy and cuddly looking and had a pot belly. Hugh, slim, slicked back hair, dapper – wearing his regulation seer sucker jacket and cavalry twill trousers – constantly smoked on cigarillos.

They would sit out on the terrace drinking and talking with my parents. Hugh's voice was very distinctive – almost bell like. He would close his eyes, roll his head back and laugh. I never

191

knew them as scholarly. Just as friends of my parents talking boring grown-up talk.

It was only when I went to Marlborough in the 1980s that my perception of them changed. The prescribed reading for History of Art A level was *The World History of Art* by Hugh Honour and John Fleming. Suddenly they had surnames and they were the wrong way round. A whole new door opened and I loved reading their book.

I am a practising artist and regularly thumb through my old copy – torn in places from over use. I am still a little giddy and star struck. Why didn't I pay them more attention on that terrace?